254

CONFIDENCE

Your daily guide to building unstoppable
confidence in your life, work, and relationships.

BY: EVAN CARMICHAEL

ISBN: 978-1-7751263-1-7

How to Change Your Life

I had just signed a three year deal with a CEO of a multi-billion dollar company who was years older than me and had nearly 15,000 employees. We were going to do a Q&A show together where we'd answer questions together from my audience of entrepreneurs. I was driving with my father and he asked me, "How do you get the confidence to be on par with this CEO? That you're his equal? That you're answering questions alongside him?" It wasn't in a 'you-suck' kind of tone. It was a tone of general admiration, said in a very supportive way. And I realized that the Evan of a few years ago would have lacked confidence, felt nervous. I would have felt less than, would have felt inferior.

So what changed? Where did I get this confidence from? It was from the changes I made to my environment and habits. Through my videos, I'm virtually hanging around Elon Musk and Kanye West and Oprah Winfrey and Maya Angelou and all of these successful people. I'm around them every day. And so, being around success daily changed me. Not overnight, but bit by bit... Day by day... I grew stronger... I changed.

By hanging around greatness more, you unleash a little bit more greatness inside of yourself. And the more consistent you are with that, the more of your greatness will come out. Now, you may not have these people around you. I didn't either. This book gives you your daily injection of greatness. This book will bring you confident, successful people that will unleash that inner boldness in you. This book will get you in the habit of learning from the greats, every single day. And they will change you. It'll happen automatically. You will become greater.

The fastest ways to change your life are to change your environment and change your habits. That's it. That's the biggest difference between you and the people you look up to. They have a different environment and different habits. You can get what they have if you change what they changed.

You are a product of your environment and you are what you consistently do. If you're around a peer group that pushes you forward, you will go forward. If you're taking consistent action every day, you will get better. This book is your peer group and will challenge you to act daily. It's not about taking one huge action. You don't change overnight. It's about taking small actions every day. That's why I don't want you to read this like a book. You'll be tempted to... You'll want to skip ahead and read multiple days at once... But please know this: Reading one day at a time and acting will give you so much more benefit than reading seven days at once and then not coming back to the book until next week. You are what you consistently do, not what you do once a week or once a month. You don't need to do anything heroic. Just read one day each day and act.

I know you've felt moments of inspiration, moments of boldness and unstoppable-ness. If you wake up and you add this daily practice of reading one story from this book to your routine, and it makes you feel bold and unstoppable... If you did that every day for the next 254 days your life will be unrecognizable from where you are today. Unrecognizable.

Now, when you read a day from this book, you're going to see a prompt to take action. These actions are designed to challenge you, push you, and make you grow. Stop waking up like an accident and make reading a day from this book part of your morning routine that has intention built in.

This is the start of how you change yourself. You're about to embark on an incredible journey... And if you can read each day, not take a day off, and do the exercises, you will come out on the other side a transformed person. I'm so excited for you to meet your future, more confident, bolder, unstoppable self.

Much love,

Evan Carmichael
#Believe

Why 254?

According to the European Journal of Psychology, it takes 18 to 254 days of taking action to form a habit. The average is 66 days of consistent action for the habit to form. I made it 254 so that even if you are the slowest learner on the planet, I will be there with you, every step of the way, and if you do the work you will change.

The 254 series is a pep-talk every day. It's like having your own personal coach give a thought-provoking and inspiring message to you, every day, for 254 days, so you can form the habit you need to go to the next level.

Please don't read this book like a normal book.

Read one story per day, use the box at the top right of each page to check off your progress, and do the exercise for each day.

Shift your mindset.

Act.

It's time to take charge of and change your life.

Share Your Progress!

Every day, **check the box at the top right of the page**, do the exercise at the bottom, and then share your progress to feel the momentum. Post an update on social media with the hashtag **#254Action and tag me**. I want to hear how you're doing, and there's a whole community online out here to support you!

Day 1: ☐

Tony Robbins

"All of us have an identity for ourselves, a way of defining ourselves. Human beings don't usually stray from that. So if you consider yourself to be a conservative person or a shy person, I know the ways you move. I know the facial expressions, the gestures, the way you use your body. That's all consistent with the fact that our strongest drive as human beings is the need to stay consistent with how we define ourselves.

The fastest thing you can do to change your experience would be to erase. The minute you go, 'I'm shy,' go, 'erase.' That's a B.S. story, B.S. meaning belief system. Now that's just a story. And if you tell yourself a story long enough, you start to believe it. Once you believe it, you act like it. When you kept calling yourself shy, you believed it. Up until this moment. Do something that's completely outside what you would normally do. Become somebody else. Decide who's the most playful, passionate, outrageous, fun person you know, and behave like them for two or three days. Just push yourself to behave like that.

And here's what's happens: It'll be shocking. It'll be weird. It'll be different. You'll feel uncomfortable. But after a while, you'll get reinforced. It's like if you get a nice haircut, you make a change in the way you look, people will compliment you. You'll get some compliments, and those compliments will make you want to use those other parts of yourself."

DO THIS TODAY: What parts of your identity would you like to erase and do over? What B.S. (belief system) story about yourself do you want to change? Write it down, then write down the name of someone you know (doesn't have to be personally) who you could behave like today. Think like that person, then write down what happens. Did you change your outlook? #254Action

Day 1 High Five!

You made it through day one, that may not seem like a huge step but starting is the hardest part! So give yourself a High Five (and remember to also **check the boxes in the top corner each day** so you can keep track of your progress).

Day 2: ☐
Tom Cruise

☐   "You have a voice. It's just getting your own confidence, and you find it just by doing it.

We're constantly looking at life. What is it? It's a daily adventure. You have your voice. It's there. Just do it. Do it. Do it. Do it. Create. Don't let anyone stop you from being creative. You do it. And that confidence will come.

There is no 'right' way to do it. There's no right way. You do have your voice. It's there. And it's a matter of you just finding that confidence."

DO THIS TODAY: When was the last time you set aside time to really listen to yourself? Take 15 minutes to find your voice and what it has to say. Do some deliberate daydreaming – whether it's in the shower, going for a walk, sketching on a page – and give your voice a chance to come out, give your brain space to produce some really great ideas – WITHOUT your inner critic interfering. #254Action

Day 3:
Eric Thomas

"I have boundaries. Just because it's my company, it doesn't mean I can take calls all day. You can't call me at a certain time. Why? I'm working. With entrepreneurs, they feel like because they own their day, they can spend it like they want. You cannot spend it like you want to! If you're working for IBM or you're working for Ford, you couldn't be on the phone all day at a major corporation. So why do you allow yourself to talk on the phone when it's your business? One of my rituals is, when I get started, there are no interruptions. I don't care if it's my wife, my children, they know that for a certain time frame I'm going all in and I can't go all in and answer the phone. I can't go all in watching TV. I can't go in with the distractions.

So some entrepreneurs are like, 'Why am I not blowing up?' Because you're not in abstraction. You don't have that moment of your day. I don't care if it's two hours, four hours where you shut the entire world out. No Twitter, no Facebook, no nothing. Just for two hours I'm going in. Once I come out, then we can do Instagram and, I'll be honest, your content would probably would be stronger if you had that time of isolation, of solitude where you give yourself a chance to think. You give yourself a chance to go in, and when you go in, you go 120%."

DO THIS TODAY: Look at how you structure your day. Where can you establish time to go "all-in" and achieve a state of abstraction? #254Action

9

Day 4:
Iyanla Vanzant

⸮   "When we think we are unworthy, it means that for some reason we believe we have to prove we have a right to our space on the planet, in life, as we are, being who we are. That means that we will do all manner of wonderfulness to prove we deserve to be here. Usually some of the common things we do are overcommit, over-give, overdo, over-excuse, overcompensate, and we stay in difficult, desperate, hurtful, harmful situations much longer than it is wise or productive to do so.

Worth. What is it that you expect from the world in response to who you are? It's very different from value. Self-value means how you hold yourself within yourself, and what you expect as a result. In order to get to the worth, if you're not holding yourself within yourself as worthy, then what you expect from the world is surely going to hurt you.

DO THIS TODAY: Try this exercise from Iyanla: "Start every morning with "I am" statements. "I am love. I am beauty. I am peace. I am joy. I am power. I am worth. I am value. I am truth. I am life. I am well." Whatever it is. Write it as a noun not as a verb. Not "I am loving" or "I am lovable." I am love. I am power. "I am." It will restore your worth." #254Action

Day 4 High Five!

It takes people four days on average to finish a season of a popular Netflix show. You've spent the past four days investing into yourself instead. That's definitely High Five worthy!

Day 5:
Evan Carmichael

"People are afraid to step out of their box. As kids, we try a lot of stuff. We have curiosity and somewhere along the line, as we get older, we get fearful. We're afraid of trying something new. We're afraid of making a YouTube video. We're afraid of getting on a motorcycle. We're afraid of going on that trip. We come up with practical reasons why we can't do something, but the real reason is fear. When I am afraid of something, when I want to say no because of fear, I try to force myself to go out and do it. I exercise that muscle consistently so it gets stronger and stronger and I continue to build and grow myself.

The hardest decision of all for me was turning down a high-paying job out of university to start this business that's making $300 a month. To say no to that, to do this company, which I didn't know if it would take off or not, making that tough call... it was one of the hardest decisions of my life. However, making that tough decision helped me make the next tough decision, which helped me make the next, and the next. So, when there is a hard decision ahead of you, don't run away from it. Say yes! Dive into it. It makes you stronger and helps you tackle the next situation, and gives you more confidence."

DO THIS TODAY: Do something today without knowing the result. Don't let fear and anxiety about the unknown stop you before you even begin. Hang in there and see it through until it's done. #254Action

Day 6:
Lilly Singh

"Feel confident. Dress to impress yourself. When you leave the house, look at the mirror. Look at yourself, and if you don't go, 'Damnnnn,' then you need to change.

Feel like a million bucks and that doesn't mean you have to spend a million bucks. You don't need that Gucci, Gucci, Fendi, Fendi, Prada, Prada. You can be rocking that straight 725 from Walmart and still be hella hot.

I'm saying make sure when you leave the house you're dressed in an outfit that you feel confident in. If you're worrying about your crack showing and your boob popping out and your pants being too tight or too loose, you're not going to feel confident. You need to feel sexy. You need to feel hot. You need to feel smoking. And everyone is beautiful in their own way."

DO THIS TODAY: Do your looks line up with how you feel about yourself? How can you change how you take care of your appearance so you look and feel more confident? Consider everything – your outfits, your accessories, your physical fitness routine, your beauty routine, your skincare regimen. Now think of someone who looks great and appears confident in a way you admire. How can you make small changes to your routines to feel more confident, to feel satisfied when you look in the mirror? #254Action

Day 7:
Gary Vaynerchuk

"Patience and failure. They all ladder up to one thing, which is insecurity. The reason people don't put themselves in a position to fail, the reason people aren't patient, is that they value other people's opinions too much, which then dictates their behavior.

My advice is, don't hold onto the thought of, 'In case it fails,' because you just need to realize it's your scarlet letter. Literally, the reason people are scared always is the outside force. Having a failing business and everyone's like, 'Oh see. You could never do.'

It just doesn't matter. And even if it didn't succeed... What? They're such better people? I'm such a better person to other people because I can build a business? That's bull."

DO THIS TODAY: Think about the last time you changed your plans because you thought, "what if it fails?" or because you worried about what somebody else said. What are you going to do next time this happens to you? #254Action

Day 8:

Amy Schumer

"*I Feel Pretty* is about a girl who has really low self-esteem and she feels invisible, and then she falls off her bike in SoulCycle and all of a sudden sees herself as a gorgeous supermodel, and everything changes for her. It's about learning to love yourself, which is what makes somebody the most attractive.

And it's true. Everybody has some kind of dysmorphia, like they think they're too fat when they're too skinny. So if you just actually believe that you're beautiful, what's wrong with just believing and knowing that? Because it's confidence. It's all mental. And your confidence should come from who you are and what you do and you need to do the work to love yourself. And then you feel great!"

DO THIS TODAY: If you're unsatisfied with your looks or anything else that could lower your self-esteem, what can you focus that you actually like about yourself? Your voice, your smile, your taste in shoes? It could be anything. While it's good to think about the things you can change, also consider what you don't need to change about yourself, why you're already great, and focus on noticing those things and feeling confident about them. #254Action

Day 9:

David Goggins

"People always say, 'Man you cuss all the time. Why?' Well, it's the best way for me to get how I feel across. I can't sit here and say, 'You know what? I went through hell week and man, it was really hard.' No that s*** takes your damn soul, rips it inside out, and then they say, now we're going to effing start. It allows me to express.

If I don't give you all of me, why the hell am I here? How will you learn from me? People take so much offense to me. You will never learn from people if we always tap dance around the truth. We tap dance around the truth by finding the right words so I don't hurt you because you have thin skin. No. Tighten up people. It's okay. Trust me. It's okay. You might be called n***** one day. It's okay. You might be called some f*****. It's okay. Let 'em call you that.

What are you going to do now? They don't own your life. How are you going to control that now? How are you going to flip it upside down and say, 'Roger that.' Now I'm going to harness this and you'll read about me years from now. Thicken your skin. Become more of a human being. Don't be afraid of the reflection in the mirror because that's all you can be afraid of. Once you overcome the reflection in the mirror, you've done it."

DO THIS TODAY: This book may be censored, but you don't have to be. Pick your favorite curse word and yell it at the top of your lungs. #254Action

Day 9 High Five!

9.5 million Americans eat at a fast food restaurant at least once per day. You're doing something better and worth celebrating. You're digesting knowledge to build yourself once per day. High Five!

Day 10:
Tony Robbins

"Emotion is created by motion. If you want to change the way you feel, have you ever tried to do it with your head? I'm happy, I'm happy, I'm happy, I'm happy, I'm happy. Your brain goes, 'BS, you're not happy!' But if you change the way you move your body radically enough, your voice, your face, your movement, your biochemistry changes. It's not a pump up. It's a true biochemical change. Sit up in your chair, show the people beside you what a peak state looks like by your example. Just show them. If you find your passion, you're going to have this tremendous energy, this sustainable energy, but momentum requires you always do the next thing to keep the momentum going.

The reason you get yourself in a passionate place is so that you change your life and the only thing that changes your life is making a decision. So while you're in this passionate state, that's where you make decisions. You don't make decisions when you're like, 'I don't know, what do you think? All right, let's decide.' If you make a decision in a state without momentum, if you make a decision from a place where there's no passion you are not going to get momentum. It'll kill momentum. It's decide, commit, and resolve.

In the past you've gotten momentum, you've gotten passionate, you've even made a decision but, a decision is the first step. Decision is like a war. I have to do this or that. All right, I'm going to make myself do this. But, commitment is when you know, after you've decided you commit to do this for the long term, whether it's hard or easy doesn't matter. You're doing this. It takes it from this moment and it carries you to the future even when things are difficult.

The third state is resolve. Resolve means it's done. It's done inside you so it's done out there. There's no question whatsoever. Then once you decide the only way that commitment and the energy and the momentum continues is if you take immediate, massive what my friends? Massive what?

Write down in your notes, massive action is the cure-all. If you're having a difficult time with something, your relationship isn't where you want it to be, your finances are not where you want to be, your body's not where you want to be, your business is not where it want to be.

You need to take massive action and if that doesn't work, try something else. If that doesn't work, try something else. Keep going with massive action and you will find the way because it will give you momentum."

DO THIS TODAY: Pick one decision that's in front of you, that's holding you back, and commit to making the decision today. Use the information you have to make the most doable choice and accept that there is no perfect decision. #254Action

Day 11:
Steve Jobs

"I'm convinced that about half of what separates the successful entrepreneurs from the non-successful ones is pure perseverance. It is so hard. You pour so much of your life into this thing and there are such rough moments in time that most people give up. I don't blame them. It's really tough.

It consumes your life. If you've got a family, and you're in the early days of a company, I can't imagine how one could do it. I'm sure it's been done. But it's rough. It's pretty much an 18 hour a day job seven days a week for a while. So unless you have a lot of passion about this you're going to not survive. You're going to give it up.

You have to have an idea or a problem or a wrong that you want to right that you're passionate about. Otherwise you're not going to have the perseverance to stick it through. I think that's half the battle right there."

DO THIS TODAY: Are you pursuing something you're willing to throw yourself behind, and put all your effort into? If you're not feeling passionate about your work, take 15 minutes to write down your thoughts about what you could be doing instead. #254Action

Day 12:
Steven Spielberg

"It was a lot harder to get started when I was growing up and wanting to be a movie director, almost at 12 years old. It was hard then, because to make movies you had to pay for film and pay for developing of the film.

I had to go to my Dad to say, 'Dad, I'll earn some money but I can't earn all the money, because I go to school. I can't get a job to earn the money to pay for all this equipment.' So my Dad helped me.

However, today it's easier. Everybody has access to a high-quality digital camera and it's a lot easier to get your hands on editing software and go out and make a movie and tell a story. It's easier today for young people to at least prove to themselves it's what they want to do for the rest of their lives, or at least in the interim for the rest of their lives.

If you get bitten by that bug, you can make a lot of little movies and somehow those films will get seen by people hopefully, that will hire you to do a music video someday, or a TV commercial, or a television show, or a someday a feature film."

DO THIS TODAY: Is there something you wanted to do as a child that would be a lot easier to accomplish today? Are you still interested in it? How can you start doing it right now with the resources available to you? #254Action

Day 13: □
Kevin Smith

"I go into the emergency room and there's my father, laying on a gurney, dead. Motionless, quiet, no breathing whatsoever. You always know eventually your parents are going to go, but I wasn't ready. I wasn't ready for that moment. My brother goes, 'Dad died screaming.' I said, 'What do you mean?' He's like, 'Well, he woke up and he was kicking the sheets off and screaming about being on fire. And he was so hot, and so hot, and get him water, and screaming. The screaming reached a fever pitch, and he died. Dad died screaming.'

That hit me like a Mack truck. I remember thinking, 'Oh, my god, in this world, where even a good man like my old man is going to die screaming, there is no point in not trying to achieve every dream that I have.' This is my eventual end. I really felt like this is my future. We're all probably going to go out screaming, so the best thing to do prior to that is to try to pack that life with as much wonderfulness, fun, productivity. Surround yourself with people that are going to help you do that. In this world there's not a lot of support. It's a lot of negativity, there's a lot of cynicism. The world is full of why. You tell people something, they'll tell you why. Throw a rock and you'll hit somebody with why. Like, 'Hey, man, I want to make a movie.' 'Why? Why do you think you can do that? Why? Why, nobody else is doing it. Why are you doing it?' There's so much why.

You go out and you find 'Why not?' You surround yourself with 'Why not' Where you're like, 'Hey, man, I'm going to try something.' 'Eh, why not? Let's give it a shot.' People who will try to help you do your dreams, make your dreams come true, and you do the same for them. We're all in this together. And it costs nothing to encourage an artist. Anybody can do this. I wasn't born into a business, or the film business, or born with a mic in my hands. I have no discernible talent whatsoever. I have no connections to the business. We're from New Jersey. Somebody picked up the movie and boom, I was off and running. And part of that manifests when you're brought into the community, part of your job, part of your honor, part of your privilege, is to make sure that keeps going, to encourage other people. Tell people it's worth the shot. Just like Wayne Gretzky said, like, 'You miss 100% of the shots you never take.' It's always worth the shot.

Do, just to see if it could be done. Live a 'why not?' life, because we're all going to die screaming, so make sure when you die screaming, you're totally fulfilled. When you encourage an artist, think about the potential that comes out of it. You tell a dude, 'Good job, man.' That person maybe one day writes that blog that you meme out to the entire world, because it says exactly what you always wanted to say but couldn't yourself, or they write that song that you play over and over after a loved one dies because it means the world to you. All that comes from encouraging an artist. Nothing good comes from discouraging an artist. So I'm here to tell you, give it a shot. Go out and try."

DO THIS TODAY: Ask yourself, "Why not?" Write down something you're holding off because it isn't perfect, then write down what you need to do to get it 'good enough' – maybe it already is – then share it with someone, or send it out into the world. #254Action

Day 14:
Tony Robbins

"Whatever you focus on, you're going to find it. You'll even find it when it's not there. If you want to change your life, you've have to change your physiology, and you have to change your focus. How fast can you change that? In a heartbeat once you change your conditioning. It's all you have to do. And you can do it fast. You can do it with a question or two.

Try this right now, answer this question in your mind, and be honest: What in your life today, if you wanted to be, could you feel proud about right now? If you wanted to feel proud, if you didn't feel like, 'I shouldn't be proud.' If you wanted to feel proud, what could you be proud of in your life today? Your children, your health, your body, is there a problem you've faced? Instead of running from it, you've finally stepped up and handled it? How many could think of something?

And when you think about this thing you're proud of, what about that makes you feel proud? What do you focus on that makes you feel proud? How do you breathe when you really start to feel proud? What's the kind of look on your face that starts to happen when you let yourself feel proud?

Think of another area of your life that you're grateful for. Or if you're not grateful, what could you feel grateful for if you really wanted to? What about that are you grateful for? What do you focus on that makes you feel grateful? How does it feel when you're really, truly, feeling filled with gratitude?

If you wanted to be excited about your life right now, and you're willing to be excited, you're willing to buck everybody else's trend. By the way, when you're excited, does it tend to touch other people, yes or no? Absolutely.

Focus is controlled by questions. If you ask a different question, continuously, not once, continuously, you will get a different answer. If you ask a lousy question, you get a lousy answer, and a lousy state. Somebody said, 'Why does this always happen to me?' It doesn't always happen to you, but the brain's like a computer. Ask it a question, it'll have to come up with an answer. 'Because you deserve it, you idiot.' Someone will say, 'How come I can never lose weight?' You can lose weight, but if you keep saying, 'How come I can never lose weight?,' the brain has to come and answer, 'You're a pig.' Lousy questions create what? Lousy answers. Ask a better question, get a better answer. Change your state. If you get the habit of doing it, you'll have a different life."

DO THIS TODAY: Excitement is contagious and it helps you push through hard times. Write down three things you're really excited about right now. Look at the three things and consider what is it about them that excites you? Are there any similarities to the three things and whether you can inject that into the things you are not so excited about or tap into when you are feeling down. #254Action

Day 15:

Magnus Carlsen

"Confidence is a huge part of chess. That's part of what makes me the best right now, is that I have the confidence to make decisions that are slightly unorthodox, or, controversial because I have belief in my ability to figure those things out over the board, while others might consider those same things but be more apprehensive."

DO THIS TODAY: Today, do one thing you've never done before. Make a decision that is slightly unorthodox, or controversial, or other people aren't doing... and you try it today. Feel the confidence it brings you to try something new and be proud of yourself for trying, regardless of if it works out or not. #254Action

Day 15 High Five!

According to socio-economist Randall Bell, those who exercised, even for 15 minutes a day, dominated statistically in every single measure of success. You're exercising your soul for 15 minutes a day too by reading this book. High Five!

Day 16:
Reese Witherspoon

"Be confident! I have to do this part. I have to do this part!

I remember going in, I read the script, and I just thought it was amazing, so I went in to meet with him, and I just looked at him, and he said, 'Hello!' And I said, 'I just want to let you know, I'm the right person for this part. You can cast somebody else, but you'll be wrong.'

About a week later, I got the call, and I got the part.

But I will say I feel like a lot of times people just want to be told what to do. Sometimes, they have so many decisions to make, they just want the decisions to be taken away from them and just to go, 'Give me the ball, I'm not going to disappoint you, I promise, and I'm going to work to the best of my ability, and I'm going to work hard for you.'

Sometimes, that's just such a relief to somebody who has to answer 200 million questions a day."

DO THIS TODAY: Be more direct and assertive today. Think of someone you want to work with and tell them to give you the ball. Tell them you won't disappoint them. Tell them you're the right person for the job. #254Action

Day 17:
Sylvester Stallone

"There's always fear. I even put it in Rocky III, that he's afraid. I'm afraid but the fear is the fuel that we use for over-achievement.

If I wasn't afraid, I wouldn't work as hard. Because the fear is, I don't want to slip back into mediocrity. I don't want to just say, 'Okay I want to rest on my laurels.'

I hear footsteps all the time and I know that I only have a certain amount of time. I don't want to waste it because it's gone so quickly.

Since Rocky, it's been years and I think that we're just over-achievers because we know that there's only a certain amount of productivity in a day and we don't want to waste it."

DO THIS TODAY: Today you're going to plan and schedule three breaks. Quit the impulsive interruptions to eat, check social media, or chat aimlessly. Schedule your breaks so you can be productive for the rest of the day. #254Action

Day 18:
Machine Gun Kelly

"Lace up. That means put both feet on that ground, lace up, get ready to face the world. Go out there, take it on and, and turn a grain of sand into a diamond.

It's about believing in something. Having faith in something. That's what it is. We're not trying to hear some president in a suit who can't even live his own life because he's so worried about public perception. We can't relate to that. They want to see someone doing what they're doing, living how they're living, coming from where they're coming from, and making something better of themselves. That's why they're screaming, because they see that.

I don't want to hear some president telling me what he's going to do, or not going to do, because they never do it. I don't want to hear some teacher put a limit on where my education can take me. They want to teach me to go and fix lights in a house, but you don't want to tell me that I can take my own career into my own hands and be an entrepreneur, and come up with something like this? They didn't teach you that you could do this."

DO THIS TODAY: Start believing in yourself. Write down five things you admire about yourself: Your smarts, your ability to talk to people, your talents and skills, how you look, how you act, your work ethic. Everything boils down to this: you are capable and worthy of great things if you believe that you are. #254Action

Day 19:
Evan Carmichael

"Surround yourself with greatness. If you want to be more confident, you need to surround yourself with things that make you feel confident, that give you boldness and make you want to do something big and new and special and different and want to actually follow through on it.

If you look at the people in your life right now, do they give you confidence? Or when you tell them your idea, do they say that it's stupid and you shouldn't do it? Does your office or bedroom give you confidence? Do the videos you watch give you confidence?

All of that matters and you want to design your environment with intent, so that wherever you are as much as possible, from the clothes you wear, to the music you listen to, to the videos you watch, to the people you hang out with, to the conversations that you have, are built up around helping you do something great. And to the extent that they're not, I would have a serious thought about whether you still want to have those people or those things in your life. If you want to boost your confidence then you need to have things around you that make you feel confident consistently."

DO THIS TODAY: List four things in your life that directly impact your confidence: two for "giving confidence" and two for "taking away confidence." Start by making one change in your life to remove something from that second list. #254Action

31

Day 20:
Jada Pinkett Smith

"Every day, when I wake up, I go into meditation. I ask for guidance from the intangible powers and I get focused. I think about, 'What does Willow need today? What does Jaden need today? What does Daddy need today? And, Jada, before the day is done, you better make sure that you take care of yourself.' And that's a new thing for me. I had forgotten how to take care of myself. When you stop taking care of yourself, you get out of balance and you forget how to take care of others. You have to take care of yourself in order to have the alignment and the power to take care of others because it fills the well.

What I do takes so much energy, so much work from heart, spirit, and creativity, that I have to be responsible enough to take care of me. If I'm not, imbalance comes and I start making you responsible for my happiness. A lot of times, we look to our men and we go, 'You! I've given all this up for you! You have to make this right by me! You're supposed to make me happy!' Because we've lost our way on how to make ourselves happy. So I had to learn how to get more balanced, and each day, I get more and more and more in balance. I get more and more happy. The more happy I am and the more fulfilled I am, it works for the family. And when I'm not, it doesn't. It's really that simple."

DO THIS TODAY: What will you do today to take care of yourself? Take 15 minutes today for yourself to get back into balance. What will you do just for you today? #254Action

Day 21:
Gordon Ramsay

"It takes years to become a great chef. What you need to do is establish confidence in yourself. Cooking is an amazing journey and don't think you can learn it within three or four years.

I'm 42 years of age and I'm still learning new, exciting things now that I bring back to the fold. But, more importantly, vision. I didn't think French was important at school and I kick myself now because I went to live in France for three years and became bilingual, but I wished I'd studied harder with a second language under my belt. That gives you a different culture, gives you a completely different level of confidence, learning French, French cuisine, mannerisms, and cooking in a very robust, tenacious way. Vision, and open-mindedness. It's one of the very few jobs anywhere in the world that you can travel, get paid and experience phenomenal food anywhere in the world. Brilliant!"

DO THIS TODAY: What can you get better at? It could be becoming more fluent in a language or mastering a software you use in your work. What can you do today to start boosting that skill? #254Action

Day 21 High Five!

Maxwell Maltz, a famous plastic surgeon from the 1950s noticed that after an operation, it would take patients around 21 days to get used to seeing their new face. You're now 21 days in. Are you starting to see some changes? Let's celebrate them. High Five!

Day 22:
Ryan Blair

"Nothing to lose, everything to gain. It's a mindset. When you having nothing to lose, you either are backed into a corner and you cower and you submit, or you fight your way out.

I've been backed into a corner a few times. Both when I was a kid but then also in my professional career when I decided to become an entrepreneur. When the recession hit, I had to apply that same mindset.

There's a lot of fear out there. Fear of the unknown. Fear is a trap and people are domesticated. They're comfortable. If they just realized that they have nothing to lose, these middle-class folks that think they have something to lose.

They think that their reputation with the neighbors, or their credit, or their Louis Vuitton luggage or whatever it is, is worth holding on to. If they just ventured out there, started a business, took action. They'd realize there's a better life."

DO THIS TODAY: What's fueling your fear of the unknown? List five ways you could step out of your comfort zone and pick one to do first. Today. #254Action

Day 23:

Aaron Marino

"You need to find your voice, and this is something that is incredibly difficult to do if you're not used to it.

I see some kids that are screaming at their mom and dad. I'm just thinking to myself, 'Man, that's incredible.'

Not that it's right or not that it's good, they really should be more respectful, but the fact that they will stand up for themselves in that capacity and that intensely is mind blowing to me.

Find your voice."

DO THIS TODAY: What's stopping you from feeling confident, from using your voice right now? Just say it out loud. Verbalizing your problem is a powerful tool to help you understand what's needed - without even having to find someone who will listen without criticism. Just talking through it can often be enough to help you find an answer. #254Action

Day 24:
Mel Robbins

"I know that everybody's problem comes down to one pattern you're repeating that you can't see. And that pattern is getting triggered by something that happened in your past, that left you with this emotional scar.

For me, the thing that I always, always, always have within myself is the fear of disappointing somebody. It's an old trigger. When you finally have a word that describes this thing that triggers you, that's where the power comes because now you can name the thing that was once controlling you.

If you can identify first of all the pattern you keep repeating, that makes you miserable or doesn't serve you or makes you lose your power, then you can start to go back and say, 'Where did I first start doing this and what was the experience that triggered it?' That's the root of the problem right there and when you expose all of that, the trigger and the emotional button like my 'I'm afraid of disappointing people, I'm afraid of disappointing people, I'm not worthy, I'm not worthy, I'm pissed off that this is happening to me.'

Now you have the ability to change it forever."

DO THIS TODAY: Dig deep to find that past experience that's fueling your fear. Think about how to reframe that past event so it no longer triggers you emotionally. #254Action

Day 25:

Dan Pena

"The question is, do you have what it takes to do what I did?

You never know. But no one does know initially. Up front. You have to try. You have to swing at the plate. You have to take risk. You have to be willing to sacrifice. You have to be wanting to make commitment. And just do it.

I keep saying that. I mean it's simplistic. It sounds like I haven't thought the question through, but that's not the point at all.

The point is, after 21 years of coaching and after almost 45 years of doing this myself, and being a high-performance person in six decades, I realize you just have to do it."

DO THIS TODAY: Confidence in the face of uncertainty. Sacrifice in pursuit of greatness. Commitment despite doubt. Go for a walk and think about what these things mean to you. #254Action

Day 26:
Ava DuVernay

"I was one of those ladies standing on the side and they work hard and no one ever really gives them a shout out. When I started to write and try to direct my own stuff, I was still doing publicity for other people's films. While I was trying to make my own films, I was asking for permission, pitching people, trying to get contacts and network and do all the things that don't matter.

The only thing that matters is your work. When I finally realized that, I started to make small things and try to move them around festivals and share my work. The energy behind that positive intention started the ball rolling. I've only been making films for five years. I only quit my job full-time three years ago. I was still holding on to publicity as a security blanket. I look at each year that's passed and all I've tried to do is continue to make work. Whether I have the money to make a film, a narrative, a doc, a commercial, a TV show. Whatever story I want to tell through whatever medium, short medium, TV medium, commercial medium, full length, documentary, feature. And so that's how we're here now."

DO THIS TODAY: Are you waiting for permission to do something that other people are out there already doing? Is there something you want to do with your life, but you've been afraid to take the plunge? Just begin already! What's one thing you can do today, and build up to doing it full-time? Write down the next step you could take to get there. #254Action

Day 26 High Five!

It takes 26 miles and 285 yards to complete a marathon. This process of improving yourself is a marathon and you grow by taking one more step every day. The past 26 days have been amazing and there's more growth ahead. High Five!

Day 27:
Bruno Mars

"I needed to take a shot at the big time. I wanted to make my album, start writing my own music. I'd been performing my whole life in Hawaii and Waikiki at parties and weddings and shows and anything you could think of, restaurants, bars and clubs.

I feel like I did a lot in Hawaii and I wanted to, as soon as I graduated high school, take the next step and hopefully do it even bigger. I probably had about $600 bucks I saved up. $700 maybe. I was young, my sister helped me out. She let me stay with her for a year and I got signed to Motown Records. That didn't really work out, but I had to learn. It's such a learning process and a lot of rejection.

I think people have to understand that that's just a part of what it takes to finally come up with your own album. You need to be rejected over and over, and everyone telling you you're not good enough, and to break through that. That's what it takes."

DO THIS TODAY: How can you reframe rejection? Consider that it's not a statement about who you are, just one particular thing. Think of a rejection you experienced recently and write down one thing you learned from it. #254Action

Day 28:
Dan Pena

"High-performance is anything but easy, and staying on top's even harder than getting to the top. Now I've been on the top of my game arguably for three and a half decades. I haven't had to work in 35 years.

People ask me how do I get up in the morning? I get up fired up. I'm fired up, I been high on life, since 1974.

Failure's not an option. And I do fail, but when I do fail, I am so, 'I can't believe it. There must be an error, or there must be a typo, because I'm so used to winning.'"

DO THIS TODAY: Consider your morning routine. List one thing you do that slows you down in the morning or keeps you from launching into your day. How can you cut that from your life or stop it from slowing you down? #254Action

Day 29:
A$AP Rocky

"I don't think confidence is something that you could buy. It's something that's embedded in you.

Some people gain it with success. That's just the icing on the cake.

But a poor man with confidence is unstoppable, almost invincible."

DO THIS TODAY: Today, build confidence by defining who you are by what you do have rather than what you don't have. #254Action

Day 30:
Shonda Rhimes

"I'm a writer, I'm supposed to be behind the scenes, and everybody else is supposed to be in front of the shop.

I was sort of going on and on and on about all of the invitations that I'd received, and my sister finally sort of cut in and said, 'Are you going to say yes to any of these things?'

I remember being very taken aback and saying, 'No, I'm busy, I can't.' And her looking at me like that's insane and at some point, just saying, 'You never say yes to anything.' And those words really sticking with me because she was right.

Say yes to things that freaked me out. It's the doing of the thing that undoes the fear."

DO THIS TODAY: Think of the one thing you've been making excuses not to try. Today you're just going to say 'Yes' to it. Go ahead, get started. #254Action

Day 31:
Oprah Winfrey

"I didn't go to school until I was six-years-old because I was living with my grandmother at that time. But she had taught me how to read Bible stories. I went into the classroom knowing Nicodemus, Shadrach, Meshach and Abednego. I could spell all of those words. I thought I was preaching to my kindergarten teacher. She was like, 'Who is this girl?'

I was never placed in an environment where I was ever made to feel inferior. I always felt like I'm the smartest kid in this room. And because I was never placed, never put in a position where I was made to feel less than I didn't grow up feeling less than.

It's all about what you believe. The fundamental key to success is what you believe is true for yourself. Not what you want, not what you desire. It's what do you believe?

You can say, I want to be the most successful person in the world, but if you believe there's a glass ceiling, and you're going to have a hard time kicking through that glass ceiling, you will be defined by the glass ceiling. And the great beauty and gift of my life is that I was never defined by the box that other people tried to put me in."

DO THIS TODAY: If you believed nothing could hold you back and you could accomplish anything, what would you set out to do? #254Action

Day 32:
Les Brown

"Spend more time on yourself than what you've been spending. It's very important. You owe that to yourself. I was reading a book by Og Mandino called, the 'University of Success.' Read one line, gave me a chill. I didn't have to read anything else in the book.

He said, 'Many of us never realize our greatness because we become sidetracked by secondary activity.' We spread ourselves too thin. Don't know how to say no. We find ourselves doing all kinds of things and never, ever have time to do those things that we need to do to work on ourselves.

There goes a second. There goes another second, there goes another second. We can't stop and hold time and before you know it, you wake up one day and you're behind in your dreams and your bills.

So decide that you're going to take some time to work on you, that you deserve that, from yourself. That your life deserves some primetime, because you are creating your own production. As Michael Todd would say, you are the star of your show. You are the director. You're writing the script. And you will determine whether your life is a smash office hit or a flop. You determine that."

DO THIS TODAY: Remove three things from your daily routine and see if they really mattered. Does it hold you back? Does anyone notice? #254Action

Day 33:
Robin Sharma

"Release your attachment to outcomes. One of the real reasons we don't do the things that frighten us is because we are afraid of being judged. We are afraid of failure. We are afraid of success. We are afraid of stumbling.

What I'm suggesting to you is, one of the reasons we don't really step into our heroic nature as human beings is because we're attached to the outcome.

And so just developing the philosophy where you live in the moment: You do the things that frighten you, and you don't really worry about what happens. That will develop a sense of fearlessness and a sense of bravery."

DO THIS TODAY: Stop worrying. Stay in the present and know that worrying about the future doesn't keep you safe or change the outcome. Think in the "for now" and not the forever. So right now, in this moment, as you read this – what do you want? #254Action

Day 33 High Five!

33 is the longest winning streak in NBA history, achieved by the 1971-72 Los Angeles Lakers. Their star player was Wilt Chamberlain. Well you're now 33 days in and on your streak. Stay consistent, every day, and you will become the Wilt Chamberlain of your industry too. High Five!

Day 34:

Evan Carmichael

"Take small steps. One of the biggest things that I've found in trying to tackle big projects is I'm starting here and want to get there. It's a big gap, and because it looks so big, I don't have the confidence to do it.

Like, 'Oh who am I to be able to go out and do that? That's such a big task. I can't do it.' All the negative self-talk starts to come in.

Where if you realize that you can take small steps, that this is really big but here to here is not so big. It's scary but not that scary. I think I can, kind of, do that. And then another step, another step and you slowly work your way up. Realizing that any big endeavor is the collection of a lot of small steps that came before it.

Trying to break down whatever that big thing is that you want to do, that seems so scary and crazy and out of this world and not possible and not within your skillset or ever going to happen for you... find whatever the smallest first step is and then the smallest next step is and continue to build those steps and when you look back, you'll have realized that you've made some pretty significant progress!"

DO THIS TODAY: Instead of keeping New Year's Resolutions, try New Month resolutions to achieve your goals faster. How can you break them down into more achievable parts? #254Action

Day 35:

Tony Robbins

"I've taught for decades that, trying to do that in your head, to be more assertive, it's hard because your brain's like, 'Oh yeah, but what if this, what if that, and who am I to do this?'

The mind plays these games. If you see someone who's depressed, without me telling you anything, you could tell me that person has a physiology to them, a way of using their body. What's their posture like? Slumped. Where's their head? Down. Are they breathing full or shallow? You know shallow. Do they talk really loud and fast? Or more quiet and more hesitant?

In order for us to feel any emotion, anger, frustration, uncertainty, excitement, we have to use our body a certain way. Emotion comes from motion. So, most of us have habits of using our body, our breath, our movement, our facial muscles. We have 80 different muscles in our face. Eight-zero, 80!

If you want to change your life and you want to be more assertive, get around more assertive people and model them. Take on their posture, move. It seems artificial... Stand with your hands on your hips, standing straight up, because if you stand that way for two minutes like Superman or Wonder Woman, within two minutes the testosterone in you, male or female, increases an average of 20%, and the cortisol which is the stress hormone that stresses you out drops 15%, in two minutes. All you're doing is standing like this and you're one-third more likely to take action, be more assertive, and do something you normally wouldn't do.

DO THIS TODAY: Take Tony's challenge. Right now, stand up like you're Superman or Wonder Woman for two minutes. See how do you feel afterwards. Are you feeling more assertive? Do you have less stress? #254Action

Day 36:
Peter Voogd

"Everyone has what's inside them called a confidence account and here's the scary thing: At every moment, you're either helping or you're hurting your confidence. There's no in-between. Every decision you make is either helping the account or hurting it. Every accomplishment and everything you've done up to this point is because of that account. I didn't realize that a lot of things I was doing, whether it was sleeping in, or validating, or making excuses, they were hurting my confidence. If you don't have confidence, there will always be a way to lose in entrepreneurship. You have to understand how important confidence is and protect it at the highest level.

Confidence is just certainty, right? What's the number one reason people won't leave their corporate job to entrepreneurship? They're scared because they have what at their other job? They have certainty. In this new economy, the only certainty you have is the confidence in yourself and your ability to make it happen. So you have to create certainty for your life and business by doing your due diligence, by studying, by reaching out to high-level people, and by making sure that you have an identity that whatever you say, your actions follow. Because when you get results, that's the ultimate confidence booster."

DO THIS TODAY: Often we don't notice or celebrate the little wins. Think of one thing that was a 'win' for you that you didn't take the time to celebrate. Should you have? Can you do that now? #254Action

Day 37:

Jeff Bezos

"The best defense to speech that you don't like about yourself as a public figure is to develop a thick skin. It's really the only effective defense.

You can't stop it. You are going to be misunderstood. If you're doing anything interesting in the world you're going to have critics.

The only way, if you absolutely can't tolerate critics, then don't do anything new or interesting. And then you can insulate yourself."

DO THIS TODAY: Think of someone who made you feel angry or upset recently, and write down six ways to turn their criticism into a source of strength. #254Action

Day 38:

Michael Gervais

"If we unpack how confidence works, it's pretty simple. Confidence comes from one place and one place only. Most people believe that confidence comes from past success and that's not accurate. It comes from what you say to yourself. At any given point in time, we're having a conversation with ourselves. If we're saying things that are beating ourselves up, it might make us better, it might. But you might not enjoy who you are when you arrive there. In time, in the dialog that we have with ourselves, we're speaking in ways that are either building confidence or destroying confidence. Confidence comes from what you say to yourself, and becoming aware and mindful of your inner dialog is at the center of being able to grow, to be able to develop, to be able to pursue potential.

It's a skill that we can teach. It's a skill that we can develop, and if we have a better sense of it, we can guide our own minds towards those conversations that build. We are asking people to increase their awareness of their own thoughts. Now what do we do with it? We want them to guide towards a positive direction, but that's not always intuitive and easy. Sometimes it really takes a coach to coach how we think, to adjust our thoughts. It's apparent when we listen to the people we're working with and we hear how they're thinking about something. We have a grounded perspective in life. We can recognize it, we can hear that. Then we can take a moment and help them think about it in a different way. That's perspective shifting. It's giving them a very specific way to change or to shift the way that they see themselves in the world."

DO THIS TODAY: Who do you trust with your most personal thoughts? Ask that person to be your coach and help you be mindful of when you're being too hard on yourself. You might even be able to help them too. #254Action

Day 38 High Five!

About 80% of New Year's resolutions fail by the second week of February. If you started this book on January 1st, you'd be entering the second week of February now. Don't be a part of that 80%. Stay consistent. You've got this! High Five!

Day 39:
Tony Robbins

"Most people have a belief about what their real potential is no matter what you tell them. That affects how much action they take and the result. Then ironically, that result reinforces their belief.

Let's say a person has unlimited potential. But they take little action, little results, why? Because they have to start with the problem of their belief. They don't believe it's really going to happen. What happens if you believe that there's very little potential? How much action are you going to take?

Nothing, little. And when you take little potential with a little action what kind of results are you going to get? Lousy little results. And when you get little results what does that do to your belief? You go say, 'I told you this was a waste of time. Told you this wouldn't work.' And then what happens?

You tap even less potential. You take even less action, you get even worse results and your belief gets even weaker. And this sucker feeds on itself until you are in a downward spiral. It's poisonous and it's self-fulfilling.

Now what if something could happen that could come along and fill you with a sense of absolute certainty. Not like 'I believe' but when you know! If you get yourself in a state of certainty that this is going to work and I'm going to find a way. And if this doesn't work I will make the way.

Then you tap a lot more potential. And when you're certain of your potential you take massive action. And when you take massive action you really believe in something you get great results. When you get great results your brain goes, 'See I told you I was a stud. I told you this thing would work out.'

Now you're even stronger, You tap more potential, take greater action, greater results. We get momentum so it's why the rich get richer and the poor get poorer.

So the core difference in people is how do you produce certainty when the world isn't giving it to you. You go out and you try. Taking more action with a belief that it's not going to work is not going to change anything. We got results in our head that made us feel certain as if it had already happened."

DO THIS TODAY: Remember that you're amazing. You've made it this far into the book and your confidence must be growing. For today, tell yourself you can do it because you can. #254Action

Day 40:

Brian Tracy

"Self-esteem leads to self-discipline and self-discipline increases your self-esteem. That means setting priorities on your work. Saying to yourself, 'What is the most important thing I could do right now?' And then disciplining yourself to do that.

Now, here's the key, and it's the great key to success: It's called task completion. Whenever you start and complete a task, your self-esteem goes up.

You like and respect yourself more. You feel like a winner because completing a task is like crossing a finish line. It gives you a feeling of winning.

If you start and complete any task your self-esteem goes up. If you start and complete your most important task your self-esteem goes up very high and you feel exhilarated.

Your brain releases endorphins which are called nature's happy drug. They make you happy and, not only that, they motivate you to want to do more things and to do them better and to do them sooner as well."

DO THIS TODAY: Give yourself credit. Write out a "done" list of all the to-do's you've achieved lately. Take note of everything you've accomplished. Reward your brain and you'll build a productivity habit. #254Action

Day 41:
Chris Rock

"I was bused to school.

People were mean and they called you n***** and spit on you and threw feces and piss at you.

That was my grade school experience. Grade school, high school, junior high school.

There's nothing I could do about it. It made me stronger. I'm not here without it.

You can't phase me with meanness because of it."

DO THIS TODAY: Where we've been and our experiences of the past do not have to control our futures, but they did shape the people we are today. Fear of failure, people's hurtful or thoughtless words, other's actions can make us feel trapped. Remember that there's nothing you can do about it, so push through and keep going. #254Action

Day 42:
Kobe Bryant

"I was such a die-hard Laker fan growing up and just my personality, for me to ask for a trade or to go play someplace else to try and chase a championship, that's not me. That's not, that's not what my career has been about. That's not who I am.

I stay with it. Stuff that I been through in my life and been through in my career, if it's taught me anything, it's the fact that you'll have good moments, you'll have bad moments, you'll have great moments, you'll have horrible moments.

You just keep going through all of them and then things work themselves out."

DO THIS TODAY: Keep your head down and work. Stay with it. Remind yourself of a past great moment and know that more great moments are ahead. #254Action

Day 43:
Dwayne Johnson

"I get up at crazy hours.

So, when my call time is at seven, then you back your clock up four hours, and that's when I get up, and I train twice.

I'll get my cardio in and breakfast, and then I'll go hit the weights. Clanging and banging, we call it. Jacking the iron.

On a movie, I'll average probably about five hours of sleep."

DO THIS TODAY: Give yourself one fully focused hour today. Make the time. What are you going to do with that hour? #254Action

Day 44:

Evan Carmichael

"Model success. It can be really scary and really hard when you don't have a plan, when you don't know where you're going, and as entrepreneurs it's especially scary because we're doing new things, we are pioneering, we're inventing the future, we're writing a new script for what will happen, and when you don't have clarity, when you don't have certainty, that leads to a lack of confidence.

If you know exactly how to do something and you've done it a million times before, you don't have self-confidence issues because you've already done it. Like breathing, or walking, or writing a letter. All of these things you do constantly and so, it's not hard for you to do it.

But when the future is unclear, it can be really hard and so, one of the things that I found really helped is modeling success.

Maybe nobody has done what I want to do in my industry but it may have been done before, or there's some pieces that I can learn from history, of other entrepreneurs or other innovators, or other actors, or other musicians, or other athletes.

They've done something that I can take and apply it to my case, and looking at that, not only gives me the strategy to give me the plan of what I can do, but also inspires confidence in me because I look at somebody here who's done something amazing, who started with less than what I already have right now and if they can do it, it inspires me to think that I can do it too or at least I can get pretty close.

I've always found that having those stories around me helped boost my confidence which is part of why I started my YouTube channel, selfishly for myself.

The Top Ten Rules, the #Entspresso, for me to be able to watch consistently, daily, give me confidence. I look at these people and see that they were able to do great things with so little. It makes me feel like I can do it myself.

And I need it daily. I need that shot daily. At least that's me. Maybe you can watch something that lasts you months, but for me, I need it daily. I need that constant injection, and so by looking at what they've done, I feel more confident in my ability to go and execute on my vision too."

DO THIS TODAY: Pick an entrepreneur that you look up to. List the three reasons you admire them. What can you do today to model their success? #254Action

Day 45:
Charlie Houpert

"'No matter what, I will be okay.' In my opinion, this is the most fundamental mindset to charisma because so many people live their life wrapped in this sort of mental loop of what if questions.

What if I speak up, and my boss doesn't like my idea? What if I ask this girl on a date, and she says no? What if I lean in for a kiss, and even worse, she ducks away? What if I were to ask this person to go, just as a friend, out to coffee, and they said, 'Oh, I was busy that day?'

All of these sorts of things stop people from acting, from speaking up, from expressing who they really are.

Now, in the social context, what you need to realize is that the repercussions for even the worst case scenario of every single one of these are not so bad. You recover from these.

If your boss doesn't like the idea, fine, move on. If a girl doesn't want to go on a date with you, probably better that you know rather than spending six months trying to figure out which signal she's sending that indicates that she does.

When you can get that mindset that, no matter what, I will be okay, and I apply this to the social field, that enables you to act with a sort of freedom that most people never ever experience.

And that means that you can risk social things in terms of cracking jokes, expressing ideas, asking people, expressing how you feel.

That means that you can risk that more than other people. And when other people see that you seem to have this immunity to social pressure, that you're expressing who you are more, they will naturally gravitate towards you because that is a strength that most of us really, really want to have in ourselves.

The most fundamental piece, no matter what happens, is you will be okay. If you ever find yourself stuck, not knowing if you should speak up, come back to this belief. It is so critical."

DO THIS TODAY: Turn off your "what if" brain. Go out and do something with confidence that you've been too afraid to do, and remind yourself that no matter what, you'll be okay. #254Action

Day 46:
Tony Robbins

"The only way to deal with fear that I've found in my life is a couple ways.

One of those ways is to turn it on itself and ask yourself, 'What am I afraid of? I'm afraid of that? I have to be more afraid of what I'm going to miss out on, missing out on my mission, missing out who I'm supposed to be.'

In other words, if you're not going to get rid of fear, then use fear. Use fear or it uses you, it's that simple. You have to say, 'Okay, what's the price if I just stay doing this? What's the price?' I need to really get scared if I learn all this and I don't follow through.

That's something to be scared about. And then that fear will get you over your fear. It will push you through. Turn fear on itself.

The second way you can do it is to use my rocking chair test. I'm going to sit myself in my rocking chair. I'm 85-years-old looking back on my life and I say I didn't do this or I did."

DO THIS TODAY: When you're 85 years old and looking back on your life, what would you regret not doing? How can you take steps today towards actually doing that thing? #254Action

Day 47:

Gary Vaynerchuk & Casey Neistat

Gary:

"This is going to blow away people. Listening. You know, I speak a lot, and I talk over people, and I'm loud and intense, but all of my success has been predicated on listening, whether I'm doing it with my ears or with my eyes."

Casey:

"The skill I use is probably communication, which I think is building on what Gary said. I think communication is a two-way street, but being able to articulate and communicate what it is that I'm trying to communicate is something that I find I focus on all day long, every time I speak."

DO THIS TODAY: For your next three conversations really spend time trying to listen to what they're saying. Ask deeper questions to understand their thought process and spend less than 30% of the time talking. #254Action

Day 48:

Brendon Burchard

"The first enemy we all have is doubt. We doubt whether or not we're capable. We doubt whether or not we're worthy. We doubt whether or not we'll succeed. We doubt whether or not we even deserve it. It's unfortunate, because I think doubt is one of the greatest enemies of our lives and it's so easy to overcome, but most people won't practice the discipline of overcoming it.

They say, 'Oh, I'm so doubtful,' and they stop. If you have any negative recurring emotion in your life, doesn't maturity require you to face it and say, 'Hey, how do I fix this?' If you're always doubtful you can't just wander around like some kind of victim. Handle it. If you've been plagued with doubt your whole life, then face it, stop running from it.

Well, every single thing that we know from spirituality, from philosophy, from the great writers and the great texts of human culture, has all revealed one thing: where there is doubt, grant me faith. That we have to have faith. And faith does not mean be absent of doubt. Matter of fact, the very definition of faith relies that doubt is still there. You can't have faith unless there's some part of you that says, 'Well, I'm going to go anyway despite the doubt.'

So I'm not saying we have to get rid of doubt forever, and handle it, I'm saying doubt should never prevent you from advancing when you feel like advancing. That in your own mind you must say, 'I must trust in my abilities. I must trust that I will figure it out, I must trust that I can build it, I must trust that I can get some help, and progress even though the doubt might be there.'

The hero is a hero because the hero does it anyway. Even though the hero is terrified and risking it all, goes anyway. And we're all heroes in some way. We can all be courageous, but I also think society overblows courage. Society says courage has to be some big, magnificent act. But it's not. Courage is just having the belief in yourself, and having the ability to genuinely express who you are. If you're doubting yourself, the only way through is to give yourself more faith and take more action. And with more faith, and more action, comes more competence. With more competence comes more confidence. In psychology, they call it the competence-confidence loop. The more you learn and try, the more you master and develop. So, go out there, let the doubt be there, but do it anyway."

DO THIS TODAY: Turn your life goals into a story. You are the hero, and your problems are the obstacles you face on your journey. How will you conquer your enemies and save the day? Write down a happy ending and go make it happen. #254Action

Day 48 High Five!

48 is an auspicious number meaning "prosperity" in Chinese Numerology. The best investment you can make is in yourself which is what you're doing every day reading this book. Let's keep it going! High Five!

Day 49:
Mark Hamill

"One thing that gave me confidence is I said, 'There's no way they're going to cast the guy who plays Luke Skywalker to be this icon of villainy.'

So I was really cocky in the sense that I knew I couldn't get the part. Sometimes what trips you up is that you want it so bad your nerves betray you and your timing's off, you oversell it.

The one thing that I felt about Joker was since there's no way I can get this, just from the standpoint of the publicity, because years after I did it people kept saying, 'That Mark Hamill?' and they'd demand on the street, 'Do the voice. That's not you. Is it?'

But, I had the confidence of knowing I couldn't get it, so I said, 'You know what? I'm going to go in there, give them the best damn Joker they've ever heard, and they're going to really regret the fact that they can't hire me. I had this arrogance when I did it, which worked well for the part."

DO THIS TODAY: Can you live one day like you have nothing to lose? Can you do that today? What can you do psych yourself up to get rid of your nerves? #254Action

Day 50:

Stephen Kelly

"The great thing about small business is we're street fighters. We're out there with customers all the time. And everything you should focus on is doing well, learning, and improving.

I would advocate, number one, don't try to come up with the Holy Grail. Don't worry about perfection. Actually get a business off the ground, engage with customers, get the product out, get the service proposition out, and then learn fast and improve.

If you think it's good enough, you're passionate about it, and you love what you're doing, and you think there's a gap in the market, go and find out, test drive it, and then you'll find out really quickly whether it's good enough. The rubber hits the road when customers tell you that you've got the best product in the world.

I wouldn't worry too much about analyzing again, is it good enough? I'd get into the execution phase and start test-driving it. A-class strategy and B-class execution is always inferior to B-class strategy and A-class execution. Get out and find out what works and improve it."

DO THIS TODAY: Call up one customer or potential client and ask for their honest feedback about your product or idea. Learn how you can make it better. #254Action

Day 51:
Adam Sandler

"I had an amazing mom. I had an amazing dad, brothers, and sisters. My brother and my two sisters, all they ever did was make me feel like I'm good at things and even when I was terrible at things, they were like, 'You're so remarkable, Adam. You're great!'

Anything I did, I sang in the car, 'What a great singer. You're so funny.'

They just instilled me with confidence."

DO THIS TODAY: Write down three of the best compliments you've ever received and post them somewhere you'll see them every day. #254Action

Day 52:

Bob Proctor

"One of the greatest hangups that people have is the belief in themselves. They suffer from self-doubt. Many years ago, I read something. It was by Ralph Waldo Emerson. It was his essay on self-reliance. That's what we want to do, we want to rely on self. He said there would come a time in every person's education when they'd realize that envy is ignorance and imitation is suicide.

So many people look at someone that's doing very well, possibly in the same field they're in, and envy them. Do you know what that's saying? That's saying, 'I don't know that I have the same mental faculties you've got, I'm drawing on the same potential that you're drawing on, there is only one mind, I don't know that, so I'm going to envy you thinking you can do something I'm not able to do.' The truth is, if you can do it, I can do it. Envy is ignorance. And he said imitation is suicide.

Do you know that nothing in this universe would move in the precise order it moves in your absence? That's true! Everything in the universe is essential. You take any part away from anything, it's not complete. And everything in the universe moves in a very precise way. So do you see, we shouldn't even want to be like anybody else because we are unique. We are truly unique. There's something about us that you'll never find in another person, we're unique. We've got the God-like ability to think.

Now, what is self-doubt? Self-doubt is the opposite of self-confidence? Confidence comes from understanding. I would imagine you're confident you can drive your car. In fact, you're so confident that you'll be talking to somebody on the phone, you'll get in the car, you'll start the car, you'll drive, and you'll drive four, five blocks not even being aware of what you've done. It's all done automatic, your concentration is on the conversation you're on.

Now when you first got in a car, you couldn't do that. The car was probably jumping all over the place and you thought you would never learn how to drive it. But you learned how to drive it, now you're quite confident.

You're confident that you can get dressed when you get up in the morning. When you were a little boy or little girl, you couldn't do that. You had to be taught to do it. Well do you know, self-confidence comes, like all confidence, with knowledge. And the more you study you, the more you understand who you are, the more confident you'll become in your ability to do whatever it is you're doing. And you'll know that if you lack confidence in an area, it's because you lacked information in that area.

Never doubt yourself. And when you do, understand that the cause of that doubt is not lying within you, it's in wrong thinking. It's in not understanding who you are. Study yourself. Self-study. You'll develop self-confidence and self-confidence eliminates self-doubt.

DO THIS TODAY: Study something that you are lacking confidence in. Watch a video, read a book, search online. Study it. Spend 20 minutes today diving into the topic. Even with just a little exposure you'll feel more confident. If you continue studying, you'll keep gaining confidence. #254Action

Day 53:

Brendon Burchard

"We have to take more action to develop more confidence. That means we have to say, 'What is it I truly want?' and start moving towards it on a consistent basis before we know the whole plan.

People think that your decision is your destiny and I don't know about that. A lot of people decide to lose weight. A lot of people decide to be a loving spouse. A lot of people decide to do something good, but they don't. It's disciplined action that is your destiny.

Some of the best decisions in your life come after you have momentum at something and then you've gained some more perspective. But a lot of us are waiting for the perfect plan, the perfect time, the perfect person, the perfect thing, to pursue our goals or our dreams. And it's that waiting that often dampens our confidence because we're at the external, we're at the whim of the world. Maybe we get lucky, maybe that person comes in, maybe the funding comes through, whatever it is.

We have to instead say, 'What can I do to begin this? What could I do now to begin?' Because even if you begin and you're not sure, you don't have to know the whole path. Sometimes the whole stairway is not illumined until you take that first step as we learned from Martin Luther King. What is that first step, and then the staircase emerges, then we can see.

So for yourself, as soon as you take that first step, that says in your mind, 'Hey you know what? I took a step, good for me!' And then you start making better and better decisions because you're able to see more.

Often you don't know where you're going in life until you start jogging towards something. As soon as you run, you start, things open up to you. You say, 'Oh look at this, look at this, look at this.' People often say, 'I wish I had more vision for my life, Brendon.' I said, 'It's hard to have vision for your life if you've never seen anything.'

Get outside of the house, turn off the TV, turn off the computer, go see the world a little bit. You'll gain a little bit more vision, and with more vision and momentum towards the things you want, you will have more confidence."

DO THIS TODAY: Turn off your phone for at least two hours today. Stop worrying what other people are up to and let yourself be bored. Boredom allows your mind to wander and help you approach your problems more creatively and confidently. #254Action

Day 54:
Evan Carmichael

"To live with no regrets. This is the single most important thing that helped me in my biggest decision in my life: Deciding between having that dream job I thought I always wanted, and running this business that was sucking. 'I don't want to live with regret.' That's what turned the tables.

It wasn't making a list of pros and cons, and strengths and weaknesses, trying to think about it logically. It was, if I didn't do this, if I didn't try to make this company work, I would regret it. Where taking that job, I figured, 'You know what? I could always get another job. It may not be that job, it may not be the dream job, but I'd probably work my way up there and get that job' But I wouldn't have this chance again, and I would regret, not taking it.'

That fear of regret. That worry about regret. That looking at your life when you're 100 years old, and back to this moment, will you think that you will regret not taking action? That helps me bust through the fear. I'm still afraid to take the action. I'm still afraid to say yes. I'm still afraid to do it. But the thought of the regret haunting me for the rest of my life helps give me the courage to feel the fear and do it anyway.

It gives me the confidence to succeed and to at least try, knowing that the trying, itself, is a victory. Even if I don't get the results. Even if my business doesn't take off. Yes, it worked out for me. I got acquired a couple years later. It was a great scenario for me... but even if it didn't work out, just knowing the answer, helps.

Just talking to that girl and getting an answer, helps. Just making that sales call and getting an answer, helps. It's not necessarily just the victory, the win, but it's certainty.

The more that you live your life with limited regrets, first of all, you'll live a much happier life, but second of all, you'll probably do something amazing and special, and not every bet's going to work out, but you don't go off and hit those amazing goals, by playing safe, and by living below what you're capable of."

DO THIS TODAY: What's one thing you have been putting off that if you don't eventually do, you know you'll regret it? Decide today to take action on it and do something about it. #254Action

Day 55:
Tony Robbins

"If you're going to speak effectively, you have to know way more than you're talking about.

This is often difficult for beginning lecturers at university because they'll do a lecture on a topic but they only know as much as they're saying in the lecture and they get stuck to their notes because of it.

You want to know 10 times as much as you are saying in the lecture and then you can specify a stepping path through it and elaborate with the other things that you know. To do that you have to do a lot of reading.

But you also have to do a lot of reading because that's where the synthesizing comes."

DO THIS TODAY: The next time you have to present in front of people, turn performance anxiety into performance energy. Try running through what's stressing you out and how you can prepare for those moments. The more you prepare going in, the more confident you'll feel. #254Action

Day 56:
Lloyd Blankfein

"You get criticized and you have to have a thick skin.

I've been there and you don't buy a thick skin. You don't even know you have it until somebody starts to try to puncture it and then you discover what you're made of."

DO THIS TODAY: Next time someone else judges you, grow from it. Instead of seeing it as a negative, trick your mind. Tell yourself this is perfect. This is your opportunity to build a thicker skin so that you're capable of handling even more. #254Action

Day 57:
Kobe Bryant

"Follow your passion first. First, first, first, first, first. When I retired from the game, I sat there asking all the wrong questions.

What's the biggest industry I could get into? Just all the wrong stuff. You have to sit there and ask yourself, 'Okay, what am I truly passionate about? What do I enjoy doing?' And when you feel that way, you feel like you have never worked a day in your life.

It's the most fun thing in the world. You get up in the morning excited about what you're doing and you have to be really honest with yourself about it. If you wake up in the morning and you're dreading going to work, do something else. Do something else.

Those are hard decisions to make but when you make those decisions, it's a very liberating experience and you'll find out that the rewards will come."

DO THIS TODAY: Stop, take a moment, and remind yourself of what you're passionate about. To follow your passion, you have to know what it is. And to stay hungry, you have to remind yourself about what it is every single day. #254Action

Day 58:
Kurt W. Mortensen

"Whatever it takes. Everyone's a little bit different. Some people do affirmations. My early mentor Brian Tracy, he was a big sales guy. He taught us to think, 'I'm the best, I'm the best.' You know that just didn't click for me. So I just turned it around to 'They owe me money, they owe me money.' And that worked for me. Some people visualize the sale, some people having a little ritual to get them into the game. For some people it's being prepared and knowing your material. It might be all of the above. Everyone's a little bit different here. Some people listen to music, some people pace. I don't care, but you find the two or three things that work for you, you get in that zone, feel influential and become influential.

I would remember past victories. I know for everyone visualizing them saying 'Yes,' visualizing getting the sale, works for pretty much everybody. That's what interesting about mindset and self-persuasion. If you're stuck on worry, it's because your vision's not strong enough. You're worrying about what if they say no? What if they don't agree? What if they don't do it? For everyone that I've ever met, visualization works. When you can see yourself doing it, it works. Because the universe will not reward you physically until you can see it mentally."

DO THIS TODAY: What's one thing you are worried about right now? Close your eyes and visualize it working out. Visualize people saying yes to you. Visualize getting the outcome you want. Do it now. #254Action

Day 59:
Evan Carmichael

"Know your One Word. Having the self-awareness to understand what it is that you stand for makes the difference between taking confident action and being trapped by indecision.

My One Word is #Believe and I know that this is what I stand for every day. When I wake up I remind myself. I remind myself what #Believe is. I remind myself how it breaks down to the credo of passion, of self-confidence, of impact, and I look at that and it's inspiring.

I don't wake up every day coming out of bed and say, 'Everything is amazing, oh my God, what a beautiful day!' I wake up and I'm tired. I'm wiping my eyes. I just woke up. Maybe some people are just fired up immediately but for me it takes a little bit of time to get into it so understanding my core value and understanding the kind of person that I want to be really helps me get up and start taking some action.

If you don't have the self-awareness, if you don't understand your values, if you don't know what you stand for or stand against, if you don't know the person you want to be, then it's easy to do nothing. Having that clarity allows you to take action with confidence."

DO THIS TODAY: Find your own One Word. If you haven't read the book yet, order it today. It's one of the most important exercises you will ever do in your life. #254Action

Day 59 High Five!

59% of all links on social media aren't actually clicked on, according to Microsoft Research. Most people are pumping out spam and aren't sharing anything of value. You're investing in yourself so you can be a force for good for yourself, the people around you, and the world. High Five!

Day 60:
Ralph Smart

"I get over a thousand questions, every single day, from people who have low self-esteem. A lot of them are models, actors, people who you might consider to be extroverts. I've even had a low self-esteem for a little while. This can affect any single person on planet Earth. It starts with this: Are you someone who allows other people to give you value? Once I stopped letting other people give me a self-evaluation, low self-esteem was never an issue again. Are you always at the mercy of other people? Goodness gracious, it must be a nightmare! That is one of the biggest catalysts for your low self-esteem. Start having unconditional, positive, self-acceptance. Most of us, we don't accept ourselves. We wait for other people to accept us before we actually say, 'Okay well I'm good enough.' No, you were good enough way before I or anyone else said you were good enough.

How do we even begin to accept ourselves? It comes when you stop comparing yourself to other people. When you start appreciating what you have, when you start seeing what is going right in your life, as opposed to what is falling apart. My life's not perfect. But, even that bird is telling me, 'Ralph, you have a roof over your head. You woke up alive today. Life is pretty good.'"

DO THIS TODAY: Write down five things that are going well in your life and that you are thankful for. Email yourself the list and look at it at lunch, and again at the end of the day. #254Action

Day 61:
Jim Collins

"The greatest rock climber of his generation is right now on the side of El Capitan doing what will probably be the hardest rock climb certainly ever done in our lifetimes, trying to free climb the Dawn Wall, on the Mescalito side of El Cap.

A young man named Tommy Caldwell is in a category of one. He has six climbs on El Cap that have never been repeated. He is ten-X in extreme environments, and he's still alive. I asked him, 'Tommy, what is it that you have? You're not necessarily more physically gifted. You're not necessarily stronger. You're certainly physically gifted, but you're not this incredible athlete that just was born this way.' He had lost a finger in an accident and so he's doing this minus one of his main fingers.

He thought about it for a long moment. He said, 'I can remain focused on, and suffer for the big thing longer than anyone else.' And I think that's what it is for these people, once they get their hands on what they see as the thing, they don't let go, and they can stay with it, and suffer for it."

DO THIS TODAY: Think of something you enjoy working on so much that you could focus on it for hours and days and weeks and years and never get tired of it. If you're not sure what that thing is, write down ten things that you might love doing, and plan days when you're going to try them. #254Action

Day 62:
Eric Thomas

"You have to make a sacrifice. If you're going to get to the next level, you're going to have to give up something. When I say give up, when I talk about sacrifice, I'm saying, give up your current blessings. It's going to be hard! Giving that thing up, that's right in your hand, the thing that you can see, that you can touch, that you can taste. The thing that you're holding on to. Risking everything I have now for what could be.

Are you hearing me? That's tough. For an entire year, I wasn't answering the phone. I wasn't doing the entertainment thing. I wasn't going out on the weekends with my girl. I wasn't spending as much time as I would like to with my family, or my children.

Shut it down. But that might last for about two weeks before it starts getting to you. 30 days before people start walking out your life calling you out. You start losing stuff to gain stuff. You're ready to give up. You're ready to give up on great because it's good. I'm telling you to look good in the face. Look good in the face and say, 'Bye-bye.' Look at the opportunities you have now and say, 'Bye-bye' to those so you can get greater opportunities.

Are you hearing me? It's going to take a sacrifice. Everybody talks that talk. Everybody talks about going to the next level. Everybody talks about next level living. Everybody's talking until it's time to pay up. And when it's time to pay, there are people who not willing to pay.

You're going to have to sacrifice some sleep to get this one. Yup, you can't get up at the same time. You're going to have to sacrifice some friendships to get to this one. You're going to have to sacrifice some entertainment to get to this one. And the only way you prove to yourself that you really want it, when you really want it, is that you no longer hit the snooze button. You no longer lose focus when you studying. You no longer take shortcuts.

You're no longer playing games. You are willing to do whatever it takes. I'll do whatever it takes to get to that milestone. And if you don't have that in you this year, baby, I'm telling you, you're going to be stuck on average. You're going to be stuck on good. You will not get to great without making a great sacrifice.

If it was easy to hit milestones everybody would be hitting them every single day. It isn't easy. But it's doable. But only to those who are willing to give up, to go up, and you have to ask yourself this question: Are you really ready to make the sacrifices necessary to get to the next level? And if that answer is yes, I guarantee you it's only a matter of time before that dream is no longer a dream, but you are living in that reality. Make the sacrifice so that you can make the rest of your life the best of you."

DO THIS TODAY: Look at the list you made yesterday, about the thing you might really love to do. Is that thing worth sacrificing huge amounts of time for? Worth sacrificing other things you enjoy doing? Consider that before going further with it. There's no right answer here, just an exercise to help you feel confident about what you do. #254Action

Day 63:

Aaron Marino

"Be encouraging and uplifting. How hard is it to encourage somebody? 'Great job. You're amazing. You're incredible. I really like you, you're great. What a great pair of shoes you're wearing.'

Compliments don't hurt either, but I'm telling you the simple act of eliminating the negative speak and mindset is one of the most critical components of being charismatic.

'You can do it. You're amazing. I believe in you.' How hard was that? It wasn't hard at all. And how'd you feel? Exactly, amazing. And I probably looked like I was pretty damn charismatic."

DO THIS TODAY: Choose someone in your life who deserves a great compliment. Think of the best compliment they could possibly receive, and give it to them genuinely. How did that make you feel? #254Action

Day 64:
Tony Robbins

"We all want to be able to change the way we feel and emotion is created by motion. The way you move determines the way you feel. I have this deal with myself called priming. Every day I say, 'Look, you have to have 10 minutes for yourself.' If you don't have 10 minutes for yourself you don't have a life. And I am not going to hope I feel good. I just got back of six countries in 12 days. I woke up here feeling like someone ran me over with a truck. The way I did it is this process. It's 10 minutes. I put some music on. I do this massive change of my breathing which changes the way that I feel. And then I do this three-step process. First I do three minutes of gratitude, where I think of three things I am really grateful for. And I associate. I don't think of it over there. I feel it.

And the reason is, when you are grateful you can't be worried. You can't be fearful. When you are grateful you can't be angry. And anger and fear is what screw people the most. Most people want to be happy, but their habit is to be worried, pissed off, frustrated, stressed. They have a highway of stress and a dirt road of happiness. I wire myself. I've got a highway to gratitude which changes all your emotions. And then I do three-minute prayer for my family and friends. And then I do a three-minute process of the top three things that I want to accomplish. I see this done, and I feel it."

DO THIS TODAY: Try doing Tony's 10 minute morning ritual. Did it work for you? If not, how can you adjust it so you stop waking up like an accident and start each day feeling bold and confident? #254Action

Day 65:

Sir Paul McCartney

"I like the idea of a band. People said we'd get a big supergroup, loaded with stars, but I, for some mad reason wanted to go back to square one and just do it as we'd done it in the Beatles.

People said, 'Well, Linda can't play keyboards,' and it was true. I said, 'Well I know, but we couldn't play guitar. John couldn't play guitar when we started. He was playing banjo chords.' And we knew Linda couldn't play but she learned. Looking back on it, I'm really glad we did it because it was the way to do it.

I could have just gone into a supergroup and rung up Eric, Jimmy Page, John Paul and say, 'Come on, guys, we're going to do it.' But for some reason I wanted to go back. We ended up playing universities, graduated to town halls.

It was funny because I'd been in Shea Stadium quite recently. You had to hold your nerve, but then you do in life. You've got all sorts of occasions that throw you, and you have to decide 'OK, I'm going under or I'm going up.' So we just decided to get out and do it."

DO THIS TODAY: Think of an obstacle that's stopping you from doing something amazing. It could be a missing skill, lack of funds, anything. Write down five things you could do to overcome that obstacle. #254Action

Day 66:
Gabrielle Bernstein

"Don't wait. Go. Do it. Act. Now. Accept we need you. We need you, we need you. You are the 1%. You're the one percent that says, 'I'm going to wake up.' You are the light workers. You are the ones that have accepted this call in this lifetime, at this time. You have decided to wake up and are chosen to say, 'Yes I'm here to be of greater service than just to feed myself. I'm here to feed the world. I'm here to give love. I'm here to be an expression of that truth.'

Don't hold that back. Don't play small. We need you. If you are sitting on that book idea, waiting a little bit longer before you start that teacher training, or doing 10 more teacher trainings before you actually teach. If that's you, just start and the pressure will be off. I can't begin to tell you. I could cry just saying this, the day I taught Ego Eradicator I was two weeks into my teacher training and I said, 'F it, let's go!' I just went and I felt so much lift, because I just knew I felt this must be shared. I can't keep it for myself. I can't just sit in my apartment by myself like this. I have to give this! And sharing it, the pressure just lifted. I wasn't the perfect teacher and when I look back it was a mess, but I did it and I started. And in those moments when we just get to say GO, the pressure's off and then we clear the path and we are guided to the next right action."

DO THIS TODAY: Say "GO" to yourself today and do something you've been hesitating about. Don't hold that back. Don't play small. We need you. #254Action

Day 66 High Five!

On average, it takes 66 days before a new habit becomes automatic, according to the European Journal of Social Psychology. You made it to Day 66. Now let's keep it going! High Five!

Day 67:
Kevin Plank

"I encourage you, if you are sitting on an idea, whether it's on your laptop, whether it's in your garage, whether it's in your basement, whether it's in the back of your car, give it a shot!

The best advice I ever received was, find out if your product can sell. Don't let anybody talk you out of it. Give it a chance, try, make it happen.

This is our greatest asset and one that we have to continue to encourage. You don't have to go broke. You don't have to bet everything on it. But you can start one day at a time, taking a chance and seeing if you, too, can build a great company."

DO THIS TODAY: If you're a hopeful entrepreneur, brainstorm 10 ways you could test whether your idea could work. If you have some other passion in life, think of ways you could test out a pursuit before devoting yourself more fully to it. Just take that first step. Today. #254Action

Day 68:
Inky Johnson

"When you think about life, everybody wants the prize, but nobody wants the process. Everybody wants the championship, but nobody wants the day-to-day. Everybody wants to win games, but nobody wants to put in the work that it takes to win games. In the Bible, it says the laborer's appetite works for him, and his hunger drives him on. My question to you is: where's your appetite pointing?

If you have an appetite for winning, your hunger will drive you every day. Your hunger will take you to the weight room. Your hunger will take you past the opposition. Your hunger will take you past the adversity. Your hunger will take you past the trials and tribulations. You have emptied that bucket. You have given everything you had in that game.

It's a mindset when you attack this thing. That's what people miss the boat on: this game has nothing to do with skill. This game is about will. The moment that you make up in your mind that you are going to play this game and give everything you've got to it, you can't help but to give everything you've got. I've seen plenty of talented guys fold. They make up excuses. That has nothing to do with skill."

DO THIS TODAY: If you're not sure what you're really hungry for in life, go for a walk and think about that today. #254Action

Day 69:

Muhammad Ali

"This will be the biggest upset since Sonny Liston and I think it is befitting that I go out of boxing just like I came in, defeating a big, bad monster that nobody could destroy. I'm the underdog. If he hits me, I'm in trouble, like the Sonny Liston fight, but I came back and I shook the world and I got Liston.

Now it's 10 years since Sonny Liston. I'm meeting another big, bad, strong monster, knockout artist that beats everybody. Sonny Liston knocked out Patterson twice and I was supposed to fall, but he didn't knock me out because he could hit hard but he couldn't find nothing to hit. George Foreman knocked out Ken Norton. Knocked out Joe Frazier. True, I didn't knock him out, but I'm so fast and so hard-hitting, so scientific. I'm a totally different man from Frazier and Norton.

When I meet this man, if you think the world was surprised when Nixon resigned, wait until I whip Foreman's behind. I'm telling you, I'm down to 215 pounds right now. I said it, 215. I'm fighting weight already! I usually train six weeks for a fight. I've trained four months for a fight. I'm chopping trees. I've done something special. I've wrestled with an alligator. I have tussled with a whale, I have handcuffed lightning, thrown thunder in jail. Now, you know I'm bad. Only last week I murdered a rock, injured a stone, hospitalized a brick. I'm so mean I make medicine sick!

The man's in trouble. Listen, people are afraid of George Foreman. They talk about how hard he hits. The world has been deceived. You listen to me now, I've never told you wrong. The man don't hit hard. He knocked Joe Frazier down six times, he got up six times. Joe King Roman, in the Tokyo, Japan fight, the Puerto Rican champion, knocked him down three times, he jumped up three times. He knocked Ken Norton down four times, he jumped up four times. When have you ever seen the man say, seven, eight, nine, ten, count this man out? When I hit Sonny Liston the second fight, he stayed out for the count of 10. Zora Folley stayed out for the count of 10. Cleveland Williams stayed out for the count of 10. What few I have knocked out stayed down. Sugar Ray Robinson, knocked him out for the count of 30. Joe Louis, Marciano, Jack Dempsey, Jack Johnson, Archie Moore, Ezra Charles, they knock them out cold. This man has never knocked nobody out cold. He's a bully, he's slow, he has no skill, no footwork, he's awkward, and I have given him a name. I named Floyd Patterson The Rabbit, I named Sonny Liston The Bear and George Foreman shall be known officially as The Mummy. The Mummy!

Because he fights, when he's fighting, if you ever watch him in the ring, he drags after his opponent. How is a mummy going to catch me? When you're fighting a mummy, you just keep a step ahead of the mummy.

Just move on the mummy. No, mummy, I'm over here. No, mummy, I'm over here."

DO THIS TODAY: Think of the biggest, toughest obstacle standing in the way of your confidence right now. Give it a name that makes it sound insignificant, and go attack it. #254Action

Day 70:
Sam Zell

"Optimism is a condition. Being optimistic is just a wonderful gift that, unfortunately, not everybody has. And, if you are optimistic, and you can see the silver lining rather than the black cloud. It gives you self-confidence and makes you a more effective player."

DO THIS TODAY: Imagine your most confident self as the main character in a movie. Visualize all the details of how you look and feel, what you've accomplished, and what your life is like. Now create a short movie trailer in your mind featuring your confident self. Play this trailer in your mind every day and see how it improves your sense of optimism about the future. And if you want to take it a step further, you can find a theme song to help pump you up. #254Action

Day 71:
Lisa Nichols

"We validate who we are by what we're doing for other people. Who we are is what we do, what we give, how we love. You are giving the world an example of how they get to love you and treat you based on the way you love and treat yourself. Loving myself more looks like giving myself a chance. Giving yourself a chance at that thing you been thinking about that nobody else knows about. You're wondering if it will work. It's giving yourself a chance to fly. Even at the chance that you might fall. And, if you fall, loving yourself is getting back up.

You might not spring up. I got up slow. My heart was hurting. My elbows were bruised. But it wasn't about getting up fast, it was about just getting back up. Loving yourself is being willing to do that and to do it first, for you before you do it for anyone else. Cheerlead for yourself the way you cheerlead for them. Dance and show up for yourself the way you show up for them. I'm not speaking to something that I arrived at. I couldn't Google my own self-love. You can't download your self-love. You have to try it on. You have to stop and breathe. You have to listen to your internal GPS system more than listening to chatter and listening to Facebook. You have to listen to what's in your soul. Then you have to hear it. Listen and be in action. And when you fall, get up to fall again another day. Or to fly."

DO THIS TODAY: Today, shut down your inner critic, and be as loving and encouraging to yourself as you would be to your best friend. #254Action

Day 72:

Selena Gomez

"I've been doing this long enough to realize that no matter what people perceive of me, I always shine through at the end of the day. I've had a lot of people try to tear me down. But I'm here. I've always been myself. I've always wanted that. I've been graceful, and I've tried to handle myself with as much class. And it's only because I know how hard I work, and I'm not going to let any of that get to me."

DO THIS TODAY: Today, hold your head up, and don't stoop to the level of anything that tries to drag you down. Don't let yourself feel annoyed about stupid things that happen or pay attention to petty gossip. #254Action

Day 73:

Joe Rogan

"The right path to being a happy, healthy person, is to do all the s*** we already know you're supposed to do. Take care of your body. Take care of your mind. Meditate. Be kind to people. If there's this person you want to improve, what are the things you're going to do? Well the first thing is this guy has to get on a diet that makes him healthy. Vegetables. A lot of good quality protein. Drink lots of water. Start working out, and get a better sense of how this machine feels when it's moving. It's flowing better. There's less tension in it. Your mind feels relaxed and you enjoy every single moment of the day better. Step 1, everybody knows that step.

What's step 2? Be cool to people. Be nice to as many people as you can. Smile at as many people as you can, have them smile back at you. Tip well when you go to restaurants. Just do the most you can. And still manage to not have people walk all over you.

What else? Do what you want to do with your life. Don't be doing something you don't enjoy. Don't get locked into a car you can't afford. Don't do something crazy because you need the money. Do what you want to do."

DO THIS TODAY: A lot of confidence comes down to having accountability for the things you set out to do, like reading this book every day. Today, decide on another goal to hold yourself accountable for. #254Action

Day 74:
Jack Canfield

"To be successful you have to believe that you're capable of making it happen. Whether it's self-esteem, self-confidence, or self-assurance, it's a deep-seated belief that you have what it takes. Now, believing in yourself is a choice. You have to choose to believe that you can do anything you set your mind to. Anything at all. Because you can.

The latest brain research shows with enough positive self-talk, visualization, and proper training, anyone can learn to do almost anything. Now I've interviewed thousands of successful people, and most told me that they were not the most gifted or the most talented people in their fields. But they chose to believe that anything was possible, so they studied, practiced, and worked harder than others. And that's how they got to where they are. If Ruben Gonzalez – living in Texas, can take up the luge which is a winter sport – and become an Olympic athlete, and Stephen J. Cannell – who was a dyslexic student, who failed three grades – can become a bestselling author and TV producer, then you too can accomplish anything."

DO THIS TODAY: Follow this advice from Jack:

"Make the decision right now to believe that you create all of your experiences. Because you do. Let's start creating the ones you want by believing you can. It's a little strange, but accepting this level of responsibility is uniquely empowering. It means you can do, change, and become anything at all." #254Action

Day 75:

Brian Tracy

"A second way to build your self-esteem is to set goals. Say, 'if I could achieve anything at all in life, what would I like to achieve in the weeks and months and years ahead?' Then write it down. Write it down. Write it down.

Here's what psychologists have discovered: Setting big goals for yourself improves your self-image and raises your self-esteem. You actually like yourself and respect yourself more when you have big goals for your life. You have more self-confidence and you're happier about yourself."

DO THIS TODAY: Write down what you'd like to accomplish today, this week, this month, this year. Make a plan to achieve those things - stop dreaming and start doing. Write it down. Write it down. Write it down. #254Action

Day 76:
Tristan Walker

"About two years ago I had the good fortune to interview Tyler Perry one-on-one. He told his story to a bunch of small business owners. He was homeless for a while, and now he's one of the highest-paid dudes in Hollywood. Fascinating story. During the Q&A, one woman raises her hand and asks, 'We have to go through these different trials and tribulations as entrepreneurs, what keeps you going? How do you get back up and just go?' And Tyler said the most profound thing that I'd ever heard: He realized that the trials that you go through, and the blessings you receive are the exact same thing. That freed him as an entrepreneur. I stopped the interview because I had to soak that up.

As entrepreneurs, at times it's amazing, at times it sucks. And I've been very blessed to have good opportunities but it's very hard, right? And you don't want to stress yourself out unnecessarily. And what that taught me was that I didn't have to be stressed. I'm going to go through these issues. They're just lessons. Let me treat that as a blessing and we're going to move, right? When I started this company, a lot of folks thought I was way more calm than I should be, and that's because I understand this lesson that I learned."

DO THIS TODAY: Look at your life from Tristan's perspective: "Every trial, tribulation, all that stuff that you go through, it's just a lesson. An inherent blessing." #254Action

Day 77:
Evan Carmichael

"Your wounds and your failures will teach you some of the most important lessons that you will ever learn in life, if you're willing to listen to them instead of complain about them.

What often happens when we have a failure, when we have a setback, when things don't go our way? We often shut down and say, 'Well that didn't work out and so this sucks. And it's this person's fault. And I'm never going to be a success.' You start blaming other people and start complaining instead of taking responsibility and saying, 'What can I learn from this? How can I make this better?' And quite often from the lowest lows that you'll have ever in your life, come the highest highs. Because you've changed. Because you've grown. Because you've broken the mold. Because you're that phoenix rising now.

And you see that over, and over, and over again in success stories. Their greatest heights came as a result of some deep dark place. And so don't stay down in that hole. Use that as leverage to learn and grow into something new. Grow into that better version of yourself."

DO THIS TODAY: Turn a complaint into an action item. Take something you're upset about and find a way to turn it into a positive for yourself and for others. #254Action

Day 77 High Five!

77% of those earning more than $80,000 a year shower at least once a day compared to 66% across all income levels. Every week, 77% of people who struggle financially play the lottery. Hardly anyone who is wealthy plays the numbers. Successful people have successful habits. You're doing yours every day by reading this book. Keep it up and your income will rise too. High Five!

Day 78:
Charlie Houpert

"If you want to get stronger, you can go to the gym. If you're interested in learning to code, there's tons of classes that you can take. But where do you go if you want to learn how to develop your confidence and charisma? Here's something that I've done that has had the most impact on those social situations, work environments, all across the board.

For the type of person who might get into conversations, and it feels like they quickly run out of things to say, the class that helped me the most with that is improv comedy. To get up there in front of a group of people you don't know and try to be funny, let alone say anything, is a terrifying experience. And anything that pushes your comfort zone is going to help you in social situations.

But there's something that's much stronger about it. You have nothing to go off of when you stand up there. You stand up there, your mind is blank. The audience shouts out a suggestion, and you have to riff off that. This might sound like it's a very isolated incident, but that's what all sorts of conversations are. You're talking to someone and they give you a thread and then you have to riff on that. That has helped me continue conversations with people even when they start to stall. So, check out improv comedy if that's something you have identified as a problem in your life."

DO THIS TODAY: Last week we suggested you could pick a theme song for yourself. Did you do that? If not, pick your song and once you did go ahead and get up, turn it up, and dance like no one is watching. #254Action

Day 79:
Grant Cardone

"Where do you get your self-confidence? You can't find it at the store folks. Can't dress it up. Can't eat it. You can't manufacture it yourself. You have to build it. I remember being 29 years old, starting my speaking career, being terrified of people. I didn't call on anybody for a year, because I was literally frozen in fear. One day somebody said to me, 'You need to handle your self-confidence issue.' So I bought a suit, but I didn't feel any better. I bought a car, didn't feel any better. Self-confidence is an inside job. You have to study, learn, practice. You have to do the hard things. Self-confidence comes from repeating experiences that are difficult. Same place courage comes from. If you want to build self-confidence, you can't listen to the subliminal tapes, it's not going to work. You need to be more aware, you need to do more.

Start applying this in your life, otherwise you're going to find yourself feeling worse and worse and worse about yourself. You want to go walk on fire? Go do it. Is that going to build your self-confidence? I doubt it. The only thing I know for sure that will change your sense of self, is the actions you take getting in front of other people. People you don't know. People you're scared to talk to. You're sitting there trembling? Do your pitch until you don't tremble anymore. Self-confidence is an inside job, not a suit you put on, or a car you drive. This is not something you buy, this is something you develop."

DO THIS TODAY: Do one thing that scares you in front of someone. It could be something in public, having a difficult conversation, standing up for yourself, anything. It doesn't have to have a deep purpose, it just has to scare you. Good luck! #254Action

Day 80:
Bishop T.D. Jakes

"To be anxious is to have anxiety about something that hasn't even happened yet. Some of you are so worried about the threat of trouble. You're not in trouble, it's just that trouble has threatened you. The threat of what might happen is wearing you down. Half of the things that you thought were going to happen never did happen. But if you allow those thoughts to dwell in your mind, they'll succeed at robbing you of your peace, your joy, your life. All because you thought yourself into a nervous breakdown, into depression, into defeatism.

The mind is a battleground. The fight is in your mind, so I challenge you to waste no more effort wrestling with other people. Your destiny is not predicated on the decision of someone else. You've wasted too much of your life trying to change other people's mind about you. It doesn't matter what they think. God is not going to bless you by their opinion. God is going to bless you by how you see yourself. Touch your body and say, 'I believe I'm coming out. I don't know how long it's going to take. I don't know what I'm going to have to go through. I don't know what I'm going to lose. But I still believe that I'm coming out.'"

DO THIS TODAY: Write down all the troubles your mind is throwing at you. Believe you have what it takes to overcome every single obstacle on that list. #254Action

Day 81:

Les Brown

"I wanted to find out, how do the people do it that went ahead of me? What do I need to do? How do I need to develop myself? What are the resources required in order to make it happen? As I started asking questions, I started running into people who said, 'I know someone who can help you do that.' They helped me get connected with those people.

Remember, we have so much energy that can take us so far. It's necessary that you hook up with some other inner-energy that can take you to the next level. I hooked up with them. They said, 'Les, let's go!' And guess what? Here we are. I love it.

You want your stuff? It's necessary you take responsibility for it. That you make it happen. That you don't give up. That you don't take any objection or disappointment or defeats personally. That you keep on keeping on. That you don't decide that I can't make it because you can't see the light at the end of the tunnel. That's a part of the program. You've got to have that kind of courage, that type of determination. You've got to take personal responsibility to make it happen."

DO THIS TODAY: Recognize that you can handle any situation, either on your own or with outside help. What backup can you call in today to make the impossible, possible? #254Action

Day 82:
Henry Rollins

"The last straight job I had was 1981. Head manager of a Häagen-Dazs in Washington, DC on Wisconsin Ave. Making $4 an hour, something like that. I had a small apartment which I shared with an old pal of mine. I had a small record collection, an ailing VW automobile, and a little, tiny life with my minimum wage job which I liked. And I looked at my life and realized this is probably about as good as it's going to get for me.

But then Black Flag, a famous band who were friends of mine, played in New York. I took a ride up to go see them because they weren't coming down to my town. I jumped on stage and sang with them. They called me a few days later and said, 'You know, we're looking for a singer, because the vocalist wants to move down to rhythm guitar. We're holding auditions, do you want a crack at this? Because we saw you on stage the other night and you're pretty wild.'

I looked at the ice cream scoop in my hand, my chocolate-spattered apron, and my future in the world of minimum wage work. Or I could go up to New York and audition for this crazy band. What's the worst that's going to happen to me? I miss a day of work? There goes 21 bucks. And I get humiliated in front of my favorite band. Humiliation and young people kind of go together. I was used to it.

And so I walked into this practice place in the East Village. I'm standing there with the band with a microphone in my hand and they said, pick the tune. And I sang every song they had, improvising most of it. Two times through we did the set. They said, 'Okay, you have a seat, we're going to go have a band meeting,' whatever that means. And they came back like 10 minutes later and said, 'Okay, you're in.' I said, 'What do you mean?' They said, 'You're the singer in Black Flag.' I said, 'So what do I do?' They go, 'You'll quit your job, you pack your gear, you meet us on the road. Here's the tour itinerary. Here's the lyrics. We'll see you soon.' So, fairly numb, I went back down to Washington with this parcel of lyrics in my hand. I went to my boss and said, 'I'm not exactly quitting, but here's this thing that happened.' And he said, 'It's your shot.' And I said, 'Yeah.' And he said, 'Take it."

DO THIS TODAY: Think of one thing you'd love to do, but fear of humiliation is stopping you from doing it. Take some small action to face this fear today. It doesn't matter if you get a great result or not, reward yourself for the effort of facing your fear. #254Action

Day 83:

Mel Robbins

"One night, Chris had gone to bed. I had been struggling. We still had all the same problems. We still had a lien on the house, still facing bankruptcy, still fighting like crazy. I was still unemployed. They still hadn't figured out the solution yet for the business. I was about to turn off the TV, and there on the TV there was this rocket launching. I thought, 'Oh my gosh. That is it! I am going to launch myself out of bed like a rocket ship. I'm going to move so fast that I don't think. I'm going to beat my brain.' Now, here's a really interesting point: I talk a lot about instincts and inner wisdom, about the fact that you have a gut feeling. What I've discovered is when you set goals, when you have an intention about something that you want to change in your life, your brain helps you. It opens up a checklist and then goes to work trying to remind you of that intention you set.

It's important to develop this skill of knowing how to hear that inner wisdom and that intention kicking in, and leaning into it quickly. So my brain's saying, 'That's it, right there. Move as fast as a rocket, Mel.' I wanted to change my life, and I think most people that are miserable, or that are dying to be great, and dying to have more, want to change. We want to live a better life. We want to create more for our families. We want to be happier. The desire is there. It's about how do you go from knowledge to action? So, the thing in this story that's important is realizing that the answer was in me. My mind was telling me, 'Pay attention.'

The next morning, the alarm goes off and, I pretended NASA was there. I literally said, '5, 4, 3, 2, 1.' I counted out loud, and then I stood up. I'll never forget standing there in my bedroom. It was dark. It was cold. It was winter in Boston. And for the first time in three months, I beat my habit of hitting the snooze button. I couldn't believe it, and I thought, 'Wait a minute. Counting backwards? That is the dumbest thing I've ever heard in my entire life.' Well, the next morning, I used it again and it worked. The next morning I used it again. Then I started to notice something really interesting. There were moments all day long, just like that five-second moment in bed, where I knew what I should do... And if I didn't move within five seconds, my brain would step in and talk me out of it.

Every human being has a five-second window. It might even be shorter for you. You have a five-second window in which you can move from idea to action, before your brain kicks into full gear and sabotages any change of behavior. Because remember, your brain is wired to stop you from doing things that are uncomfortable or uncertain or scary. It's your job to learn how to move from those ideas that could change everything into acting on them."

DO THIS TODAY: What are you pausing on acting on today? Try Mel's exercise. Count down from 5-4-3-2-1 and then just go do it! #254Action

Day 84:
Satya Nadella

"I have confidence. One of those fascinating things I've learned is that all great achievement happens only when you have self-belief and you have confidence in yourself. But there is this fine line between confidence and hubris. I've always felt that I want to be on the side of confidence, not hubris. And to assume destinations in my mind is more hubris than confidence."

DO THIS TODAY: Think about how much of your lack of confidence comes from worrying that you'll be seen as having hubris and appearing arrogant. What's the difference between confidence and arrogance for you and how will it impact your actions? #254Action

Day 85:
Robin Sharma

"Practice bravery training. You want to be a great footballer? We understand you have to put in the time to practice. You want to be a great chef? We understand you have to do the practice. You want to be a great entrepreneur? You have to put in the hours of discipline building your business.

And yet, when it comes to fear, we don't live in a society that values bravery training. You don't really hear people saying, 'Go out and use this day to practice becoming fearless.'

And yet, we all know the 10,000-hour rule. We all know the 10-year rule, pioneered by Anders Ericsson. And that rule has now been popularized by a lot of authors.

But what he found was this: if you look at any great performer, they had one thing in common. They spent the equivalent of 10 years, or 10,000 hours, practicing their skill before the first signs of genius showed up.

So to become fearless, why not find some time every day to practice becoming fearless? Why not use whatever irritates you or frustrates you or frightens you during your day as bravery training?

Let's say, your supervisor walks in and says, 'Tomorrow, I'd like you to give a presentation on that project you did so brilliantly on.'

And start to pay attention: You notice you start to feel afraid. Develop the mindset where you say, 'Okay, I'm going to say yes, because that is bravery training.'

Let's say you go home, and with your romantic partner, you want to say something, ask for more love, ask for one of your needs to be met. But then you feel, well, what if he or she judges me? What if I get laughed at? What if they think I'm strange?

Develop the mindset where you recognize that everything that scares you is bravery training. Practice becoming fearless, and you will become a fearless human being."

DO THIS TODAY: By this point you should have practiced doing some things that scare you. Write down three things they've inspired you to tackle next. How will you ladder up your bravery training to pursue your biggest goals with confidence? #254Action

Day 86:
Kevin O'Leary

"In corporate America today... when you want to be a leader, you have to articulate your idea in 90 seconds or less.

You have to explain why you're the right person to lead. And above all, you have to know your numbers. You can see it happen on Shark Tank. It works in the real world too. And frankly, Shark Tank is the real world because it's real capital.

So I use that, and I teach it, and I think everybody should think about that: Explaining your vision clearly, succinctly in the short period of time ends up being really important."

DO THIS TODAY: Create an 'elevator pitch' that's 90 seconds or less – for yourself. Not your business, your work, or anything you do, but for who you are. Pitch you to yourself. #254Action

Day 87:
Les Brown

"Overcoming the negative conversation, that inner dialogue that's going on all the time, even when you don't want it to be there, you can't stop yourself from thinking right now. You can't do it. It's going on. And so learn how to empower yourself. Part of doing that is standing up to yourself. You've got to stand up inside yourself sometimes and say, 'Shut up! You've got to do this.'

I was going to give a presentation and this voice inside of me was saying, 'You can't do this. You don't have everything it takes.' I say, 'Shut up! Yeah, I'm behind in my bills and you're telling me what I can't do. I have got to do it.' You'll be scared sometimes. Your mind will go blank on you. Some people you will allow to unnerve you. And you'll wonder, 'What's wrong with me? I'm not crazy.'

That's why you've got to learn to make a conscious, deliberate, determined effort to stand up inside yourself. Working on yourself, watching that inner dialogue, will determine the quality of your life."

DO THIS TODAY: Make a list of five things that the next time you catch yourself saying it you'll tell yourself to 'Shut up!' #254Action

Day 88:

Hans Zimmer

"I have stage fright and I never confronted the risk until Belgium. The year 2000. You have no idea what it took then to get me to do it. I had 1,000 excuses why not to do it, and then finally I did it, and it was... exquisitely horrifying. That's the only way I can put it. It was very, very, very complex.

What was really good was, right at the beginning, within like two seconds, I played just the worst wrong note. And I could either stop and cry, or I could laugh, right? And it didn't kill me! And nobody else out there, nobody was throwing anything. You know? It was fine. Thank you to the people of Ghent for not killing me, and giving me the courage – and the absurdity. You have to be able to laugh at yourself. And you have to learn to laugh at yourself."

DO THIS TODAY: Think of the last mistake you made that you feel embarrassed about. Give it new perspective and laugh at yourself, laugh it off, and keep going. #254Action

Day 88 High Five!

Among wealthy people, 88% read 30 minutes or more each day. Habits matter. Reading this book every day matters. You're growing, learning, and getting stronger. Keep it up. High Five!

Day 89:
Evan Carmichael

"For me, confidence comes down to two things. First is having done it before. If you've done something before, then it's a lot easier to do it again. But an easy segue from that is, if you've done a smaller version of it, then you have a little bit more confidence. A lot of people have these big goals, and it looks like such a big chasm that you have to cross, that it's scary. So start here, do that little step, and every time you take a little step it gives you confidence to go off and do the next step. Because that next step isn't as big and scary as jumping all the way to the top. You'll eventually get there. And when you look back, it wasn't this big, scary, impossible thing, because you built confidence every step along the way.

The other thing that really helps me is remembering the mission, and not wanting to live with regret. Any time I'm afraid, any time I don't feel confident, I imagine myself on my deathbed, looking back on my life. This thing that I'm afraid of right now, am I going to regret not doing this when I'm dying? Will I say, 'I should have taken that opportunity, I shouldn't have been afraid, I should have gone for it?' Remembering that, having that kind of context and perspective, doesn't eliminate the fear – but it helps put it in better perspective and gives me the confidence to just push through. It's feeling that fear and doing it anyway."

DO THIS TODAY: Break down a big goal into ten smaller goals, then go out and do the first step. #254Action

Day 90:
Elliot Hulse

"You don't get rid of self-doubt through the same means by which you learned it, and that is in the mind. Self-doubt is purely a mind-created phenomenon. You were taught it, and you do it to yourself. Your heart and your guts have a brilliance to them that allow them to do some magnificent s*** without the mind getting in the way.

The fastest band-aid ripped-off remedy to fixing this terrible situation is to do the thing you're afraid to do. It's not about feeling confident about going into the situation. It's not about knowing that it's going to work out. It's not about having the most detailed plan for how this thing will happen. It's about doing it. Courage.

Courage is what you will experience and what you will grow, when the doubt is there but you do it anyway. So your problem isn't doubt, your problem is courage. Doubt gets out of the way when you express courage. Doubt is burned off by courage.

Ralph Waldo Emerson said, 'Do the thing, and you will have the power.' We're waiting for the power, we're waiting not to self-doubt any longer. Whatever it is that you're deciding that you want to do with yourself that you're doubting your ability on, just do it! Even if you fail completely.

That's another thing that you have to get through your mind: Success is not doing the right thing, and it definitely isn't doing the right thing the first time. Success is having the courage to move in the direction of your dreams. Move in a direction that your heart is taking you. That is what success is. People think success is, 'I have to plan, and I go and work out that plan.' It never ever works that way.

Success is the progressive realization of a worthy goal. But progressive realization means that you're doing things that you don't know how to do. You're stepping out in faith. You're being courageous. Your self-doubt will step out of the way when you build the guts to do the thing. And the power will be added to you."

DO THIS TODAY: You've got a goal but you don't know how to accomplish it yet. What can you do to step out in faith, be courageous, and start the learning process today? #254Action

Day 91:
Robert Rodriguez

"If you say, 'I'm a fraud, they'll figure me out, I'll never be able to do it again,' that's an artist's thought processes. You're an artist. If you're thinking like that you're on the right track because they all feel that way. So there's always some success that's going to come out. Even out of your failures. In fact, probably your biggest successes will come directly from your failures.

Winston Churchill's quote is my favorite. 'Success is moving from one failure to the next with great enthusiasm.' You should be very enthusiastic about your failures because you're going to learn something. You're going to go that way when everyone else is going the other way. And you're going to stumble. But you're also going to stumble upon something that no one ever thought of. So you just keep going and keep going. And you're going to fail, and then rise up, and fail again. And that's the journey. Up and down, man."

DO THIS TODAY: What recent 'failure' can you feel enthusiastic about? What did you learn from it? #254Action

Day 92:
Conor McGregor

Interviewer: "Stripping that all back to the start of your career. A man with a dream, training in the gym, day in, day out. If somebody said to you that you'd become as successful as you are now, what would you have said back then?"

McGregor: "'I believe you,' is probably what I would have said. Because I did believe. I believed in it. I had very few people who told me that. I had a small, small, small group of people that would tell me something like that. Other than that, it was just me telling myself. So if someone came up to me and told me that, all the way back then, I'd say, 'You're damn right!'"

DO THIS TODAY: Fast forward your life 10 years down the road. Imagine the 10 year older version of yourself travelled back in time to you right now and says to you, "You will become a massive success." #254Action

Day 93:
Brendon Burchard

"Other people in our lives don't need us to support and take care of them the way we feel like they do. Because we're caretakers, leaders, and managers, we feel like we have to do everything for them. Our mindset needs to switch from, 'I need to take care of everybody,' to, 'I need to equip and empower everybody to take care of themselves.' You don't have to cook the kids lunch every day. They can be taught to make their own lunch. Look, a kid can be taught to make a sandwich. Empower them to handle their own stuff.

And I don't mean just your children, I mean your team. Your team doesn't need to be micromanaged. Let them run with the ball. Learn to equip and empower people versus taking care of them. All of a sudden, you're getting hours and hours and hours back. Time back for you to follow your own dreams. Time back for you to sleep. Time back for you to take a bigger picture of the world, To find your own sense of creativity and contribution again, versus micromanaging every little element of your day. Stop micromanaging, start empowering, and you'll see a sudden huge shift in everything in your life."

DO THIS TODAY: Think of a task you're responsible for that someone else could do that would save you more time. Write down a plan to start delegating that task today. Build their confidence while you're building your own too! #254Action

Day 93 High Five!

93% of wealthy people say they had a mentor who helped them achieve their success. This book is your mentor. These pages are making you strong. You're on your new path. Keep going. High Five!

Day 94:
Evan Carmichael

"Find your One Word. It's one of the most important things that you can do. It's understanding what you stand for as a human being. It's your framework to make the right decisions. When you understand what it is that you stand for, you start to raise your standards of the people you're around, of what you will and will not accept anymore. It makes a big impact on your self-confidence. When you are saying 'no' to something, it's not out of fear, it's out of principle, and understanding the difference. When people find their One Word, they're happy because they have clarity but also sad because they realize how many things in their life are not congruent with where they should be. For you to realize the potential you have, you need to act a certain way that is most true to you. You'll notice how many things in your life, from the people you're around to the businesses you're involved in, to the things that you do on a day-to-day basis, are not in line with you achieving that 'best version of yourself' status.

When you find your One Word, things change. That self-awareness to understand who you are, what you stand for and making decisions around it makes a huge difference in your self-confidence. When you say 'no' to something, it's out of conviction, not out of fear of being judged."

DO THIS TODAY: To find your own One Word you can read the book! #254Action

Day 95:
Cindy Trimm

"Stop procrastinating. Focus on your goals. When you focus on what you want, what you don't want automatically leaves. Don't focus on eliminating anything, focus on creating what you want. So you're either going to spend all your energies eliminating what you don't want or you spend your energies on what you want. We all have alibis, we're all busy. Busy doing what?

I'm going to challenge you. Stay focused on your goals and if you don't have goals, write some goals. Where should your goals come from? Your goals should come from your vision. Where should your vision come from? Your vision should come from your purpose. If you don't know what your purpose is, you're not going to have a vision. If you don't know what your vision is, you won't have the right kinds of goals. So that means you're going to be busy like the rat in the rat race. And your next year is going to look like your last year."

DO THIS TODAY: Use this prompt from Cindy: "One of the greatest enemies of the fulfillment of purpose is procrastination and broken focus. If you start now and you say 365 days from today's date, this is what I want to accomplish. If you do one a day, at the end of one year, you will have made 365 steps towards fulfillment of purpose." #254Action

Day 96:

Aaron Marino

"Smile often. Fact: Charismatic people know the power of the pearly whites and they're not afraid to use them. If you want to be viewed as one charismatic mother, you need to smile.

Now, one of the issues that I hear a lot is that guys say, 'Yo, I hate my grill,' I'm here to say that if you do, if it's preventing you from smiling, save up the money and get it fixed. Braces, implants, orthodontic procedures, veneers. There are options out there. Are they expensive? Some of them. Is it worth saving up? Yes, but regardless of the quantity or quality of the teeth you have in your mouth, the one thing you can do is keep them clean and smile."

DO THIS TODAY: Write down three ways you can remind yourself to smile more often. Here are some examples: Set a notification in your calendar. Put a sticky note on the fridge or mirror. Change the background image of your computer or cell phone. Use those or come up with your own. It's time to smile more! #254Action

Day 97:

Brendon Burchard

"The thing that most people are actually fearing is what I call 'outcome pain.' They're scared of losing things to change. What if they go through all this terrifying, difficult work and then, the grass isn't greener on the other side? What if the outcome is no better than I had at the very beginning? I was terrified of that with my business too. I thought, 'Oh my gosh. What if I begin this business and I do all these things, and I work my butt off, but I don't make it? I don't earn any more money? I don't have a better lifestyle? I don't grow as fast? What if, on the other side of the fence it's not any better?'

If we're stuck thinking that way, we never change. So instead of focusing on the outcomes that are negative, we can give our attention and focus to those things that would be satisfying, fulfilling, joyous, on the other side of that fence. Things that would be wonderful and magnificent if we changed our lives. When you do that, you start to master your mind, and direct it better. When you're obsessing about loss pain, process pain and outcome pain, guess what? The more you focus on those, your brain and your body say, 'No! Don't do that! I don't want to experience that.' We're unbelievably driven to avoid pain. We have to stop suffering in our minds, and stop stewing about the pain we might experience if we pursue the very things that would improve our lives."

DO THIS TODAY: What kind of outcome pain are you dealing with right now? What are some of the positive, joyful alternatives? #254Action

Day 98:

Benjamin Altman

"Before a conversation, put your mind in the other person's body and think, 'What's good for them?' Because you don't want to be the selfish bulldog that's running through life and not thinking about other people. A conversation goes better if you think about what's going to help this person achieve their goals, what motivates them, their values.

The best story I've ever heard for this is about Charlie, who wanted to move to New York. He could have just quit his job in Washington, he could have put in his two weeks' notice, he could have done it via email, because he was really scared to have this conversation. But, instead, he got some time with his boss, and said, 'Hey I really like it here. I really like the people. But I'm unhappy in D.C. All my friends are in New York. It's important to me to be happy. I need to move, but I want to do this in the best way possible for you. So does that mean working remotely, or do you guys hire my replacement and I train them and it takes a couple months for me to go to New York? How can I do this so it's good for both of us?' They had a great conversation, they ended up with Charlie working remotely. First person of his position to do it. And he got a 50% raise because he switched from employee to contractor. That incredible outcome couldn't have happened if he hadn't thought about the other person."

DO THIS TODAY: Is there a conversation you need to have that might lead to a great outcome if you frame it to be mutually beneficial? #254Action

Day 99:
Machine Gun Kelly

"I just recently found my confidence. This year is the first year that I had this boost of confidence. And it's because this idea of what cool is, is burned into our brain. I'm starting to open up to so many more things, to see how being cool is a total facade. Even celebrity-wise, all those people I thought were these awesome people, and you meet them and they're so uncharismatic and so lame and so corny and so uncool."

It's so sad. These are the people that are making us feel bad about our bodies, or our face, or our hair, or our lifestyle, or our choices. Just spare me, man. I'm so over it.

I say take it all in stride. Shrug it off. Let them peak, man, let them peak. That's what I say, let them peak."

DO THIS TODAY: Think of the people you find the coolest, that you most aspire to be like. Guess what flaws they might have and realize that they too are human. Then write down ways that their confidence helps amplify their coolness. What can you learn from them? #254Action

Day 100:
Oprah Winfrey

"I have paid attention to my life, because I understand that my life, just like your life, is always speaking to you where you are. In the language, with the people, with the circumstances and experiences that you can understand if you are willing to see that always life, God, is speaking to you.

Now, it took me a while to actually really get this and to understand it. But once I did, I started paying attention to everything. And one of the reasons why I can offer my gatherings of information and wisdom and call myself a spiritual teacher is that every single person who ever came on my show, and I hear there's like 37,000 guests I've talked to, a lot of them came from dysfunction. A lot of them wouldn't appear to be teachers, but every one of them had something to say that was meaningful and valuable. That I could use to grow into the best of myself, which is what all of our jobs are. Your number one job is to become more of yourself. And to grow yourself, into the best of yourself."

DO THIS TODAY: What has your life taught you so far that you can consider meaningful and valuable? What can you learn from that lesson moving forward? #254Action

Day 101:
Simon Sinek

"Nelson Mandela is a particularly special case study in the leadership world. You can take other personalities, and depending on the nation you go to, there are different opinions, but Nelson Mandela is universally regarded as a great leader.

He was actually the son of a tribal chief. And he was asked one day, how did you learn to be a great leader? And he responded that he would go with his father to tribal meetings and he remembers two things when his father would meet with other elders: One, they would always sit in a circle. And two, his father was always the last to speak.

You will be told your whole life that you need to learn to listen. I would say that you need to learn to be the last to speak. I see it in boardrooms every day of the week.

Even people who consider themselves good leaders, who may actually be decent leaders, will walk into a room and say, 'Here's the problem, here's what I think, but I'm interested in your opinion, let's go around the room.' It's too late.

The skill to hold your opinions to yourself until everyone has spoken does two things: One, it gives everybody else the feeling that they have been heard, and the ability to feel that they have contributed.

And two, you get the benefit of hearing what everybody else has to think before you render your opinion. Practice being the last to speak. That's what Nelson Mandela did."

DO THIS TODAY: Next time you have an important meeting or conversation, practice being the last to speak. Here's how Simon Sinek says to do it:

"If you agree with somebody, don't nod yes. If you disagree, don't nod no. Simply sit there, take it all in, and the only thing you're allowed to do is ask questions so you can understand what they mean and why they have the opinion that they have. You must understand from where they are speaking, why they have the opinion they have, not just what they are saying. And at the end, you will get your turn. It sounds easy; it's not." #254Action

Day 102:

Evan Carmichael

"Here's what I think happens to most people: some opportunity comes along that you're afraid of. But it's going to stretch you beyond what you've ever done before. You find the reason why you can't go and do it. But deep down, the reason is you're just afraid. And until you spot the fear and understand that it's just the fear, then you're never going to solve the problem. So step one is understanding when there is fear.

Step two is then stepping into it and doing it anyway. When I was starting my YouTube channel, my agent would tell me you have to go out and do videos in public. My natural reaction was fear, but I didn't catch it. Initially it was, 'The gear won't be as good in public, I can't control the light settings, I'm going to be bouncing around with the camera, it's not going to be a great experience for the people watching... Why would I do that?' I'm rationalizing a reason why I don't have to do it, but really I'm just afraid. And he told me, stop being afraid. Just go out and do it.

So I forced myself through it. I recognized the fear and I jumped into it. And now it's to the point where I'll make videos in the streets. Saying 'no' should never be because you're afraid. You want to re-jig your system, so whenever fear is the answer, you have to do it. And you build your muscle that gets stronger, and take on new opportunities so you don't play safe and play small for the rest of your life."

DO THIS TODAY: What are you rationalizing that you shouldn't do but are just actually afraid? How can you step into that fear in a small way today? #254Action

Day 103:
Aaron Marino

"Do you use 'filler words', and if so, what are they? If you're not sure, ask your friends or family. Because if you don't know, I'm sure they will. That's exactly how I found out that I use the word 'um' all the time. One day, about six years ago, Tracy came up to me and said, 'You say 'um' all the time.' I told her to start pointing it out. Every time she noticed or heard me use the word 'um', she would say 'um.' And that was my cue to start paying attention.

But something remarkable happened. After a little while of being ultra-aware of myself, I would actually start correcting myself. It was really awkward and uncomfortable when I was having a conversation with somebody else, but eventually I stopped. It took hard work, being hyper-aware of what I was saying, and I was a little bit paranoid. But eventually, I kicked the habit. And so can you. A great tip I would give to you is when you're talking, and you feel your filler word coming on, just pause, and pick up where you left off. And eventually, you will be able to kick the filler-word habit."

DO THIS TODAY: Find out what filler words you use most when speaking, and strategize how you're going to catch yourself using them and kick the habit. #254Action

Day 104:

Evan Carmichael

"Make sure you're doing something every single day. This is something I took from Jerry Seinfeld. He'd have a calendar and put an X on it every time he took action on something. 'Don't break the chain, don't break the chain. You never want to break the chain of X's.'

I'm a big believer in momentum. Get some momentum going for you. It's really hard when you take a day off, then get back on the horse. You might be able to, after you develop the discipline, but especially at the beginning, try not to break a day. You may not always be able to spend the amount of time that you want, but as long you can do one minor activity, to just check the box, to put that X on the calendar, I think it really helps build a pattern.

The key is to be persistent and take this action. The more you build the habit of doing it every single day, even if it's just a micro thing, helps you believe that you can, and continues the momentum chain. And if you miss a day, especially if you miss two days or more, then it's really hard to get back on the train to take that action. So don't miss a day even if it's taking a tiny step."

DO THIS TODAY: If you haven't been consistent in following this book every single day, change that habit right now. Check the boxes on the pages each day by reading the page and doing the exercise. Today's is an easy one: Just make the commitment that you'll keep checking the boxes daily... and you can check today's off! #254Action

Day 105:
Marie Forleo

"Being a really, really good listener is one of the most underrated secrets to success. It's crucial if you want to be more charismatic, more persuasive, and a better negotiator.

Plus, really listening to someone and having them feel truly heard, is one of the biggest gifts you could ever give someone.

The problem is, most of us suck at listening and we don't even know it. We're always interrupting others with our brilliant ideas and our feedback and most often it's the way that we suck the most.

Now I'm probably one of the worst offenders out there, but I'm consistently working on this. Not so long ago I used it with my stepson, Zane, and had an unbelievable result.

Zane was home on Christmas break from college, and he invited me to go for cappuccinos. (A little back story here: in the 10 years plus that we've been in each other's lives, he'd never really asked me for life advice.) So we're hanging out and Zane starts to tell me all about his life and what he might want to do with it. He's very involved with music. He's involved in acting and all these creative things. He's asking me for the kind of advice that I give for a living.

So you could imagine every, single part of me just wanted to jump in and tell him what to do and tell him what I think and yada-yada-yada. But I just sat there and I zipped it. Now every time I did this and I just shut up, it was amazing because he would just reveal more and more insights, he'd find new things to talk about, he'd find his own insights that were way better than anything I could have told him, and it was really, really amazing.

Now I have to be honest, my body was uncomfortable being silent. So every time he would come to an end of a sentence, I would sit. And see if there was more. And it was absolutely awesome.

By the end of three hours, we had the most beautiful conversation and we left that cafe feeling more connected and more intimate than I think we've ever felt. So just a little story to show that it really, really works."

DO THIS TODAY: Next time you're having an important conversation, give the other person space to completely share their thoughts and stories. You might be surprised at what you'll learn, and how grateful they'll feel that you listened. #254Action

Day 106:
Charlie Houpert

"The subconscious and the conscious mind speak different languages. The conscious mind is verbal. We talk to our friends, our family, we can even talk to ourselves all day but it's very, very difficult to talk yourself into feeling a certain way. What you need to do is have an experience, even if that experience is imagined. The subconscious mind speaks in experiences, while the conscious mind speaks more in language that we use every single day. So, how do we experience something we want to embody? One of the most helpful ways that I've ever encountered, and I do all the time, is when I have a negative feeling, particularly self-doubt, I will free-write. That is embodiment. There's tons of different ways, but that's the simplest and most effective that I've found to clear out self-doubt. So if there's something you got right now, start here. If it's recurring in your life write it out, delete it, burn it. But make sure first you have that feeling of pouring outside of yourself."

DO THIS TODAY: Try this free-writing exercise from Charlie: "Open up a Word document and free-write for 3 pages. Or go to 750words.com. 750 words is about three pages and it's enough time to just type, and it will count your words for you. Type everything that's bothering you. I feel this way because this-said-that and now I'm going back and forth in my head. Dump it all. Actually feel it being poured onto the page. If you want to free write it, some people enjoy this better by hand, that can give you that feeling of catharsis. This is important. This is not just a metaphor because once you've gotten it out onto the page, onto that website, you shut down the browser, close the computer. Turn it off. There is this feeling of closure. If you have a word document you drag it to the trash. You empty the trash. It's gone. If there's a piece of paper you light it on fire. It's so weird because why would this help you? The subconscious mind speaks in experience and what that experience was, was I dumped all my feelings here and then I lit it on fire and it's gone. It is incredible how effective that is." #254Action

Day 107:
John Addison

"Most of us that come from normal backgrounds, we don't see ourselves doing abnormal things. The world is full of people who were born on third base and think they hit a triple. They've got all this confidence, all this stuff. For most of us, it's not that way. We don't think we're wired or programmed to do something great. Well, I'm telling you, that thought is nothing but a fear. Nothing but a doubt. It's what holds you in place. You have to work hard on understanding you have within you the power to change. The power to do something great. And those fears are going to crop up. When you wake up and you're scared to death about what to do, they're going to hold you in place. Quite often if you're trying something different, they crop up in the middle of your dreams when you're asleep at night. Those fears and doubts creep in.

Understand, they're not real. They are things in your head that have been programmed into you by your past life. Wrestle with those fears. You'll never conquer them, but control them, and go out and live the life you deserve. Choose to win. Control your thinking and go win big. See you at the top."

DO THIS TODAY: Find a hero of yours who also came from a normal background, just like you. Maybe even worse than you. Feel confident in knowing that if they could do great things, so can you! #254Action

Day 108:
Jack Ma

"One of the things that's so fascinating to me is that Amazon and Jeff Bezos have pursued what might be described as a very asset-heavy business model. They're buying airplanes. They want to own the entire supply chain from beginning to end. And Alibaba is effectively an asset-light business. In terms of the retail piece of this, we're very much the opposite! What do you think about that? Is Jeff Bezos right or are we right? Is there going to be a meeting in the middle? I hope both are right. Because the world can never have one model. If the world has only one correct model, the world is too boring. We need to have all kinds of models. And the people who do the model should believe in the model. And I believe what I do."

DO THIS TODAY: Consider Jack's belief that there is room for more than one model in this world. Is there something you haven't attempted because you feel someone else is doing it better? What would happen if you do it differently? #254Action

Day 108 High Five!

There are 108 pressure points in the human body, according to the Ayurveda, a system of medicine with Indian roots. You're 108 days in and have now gained a piece of advice for every pressure point on your body. Let's keep that growth going. High Five!

Day 109:
Gabrielle Bernstein

"Early in my career I was always trying to be someone else. I tried to be the cool girl, or the successful girl who had it all. But what I've learned is that to be truly confident I didn't have to try so hard. I merely had to strip away those pretenses to release the building blocks, the presence of who I truly am.

When I became more me, I started living my purpose with confidence and taking action on my dreams. And that's the lesson. All the world wants from you is your authentic truth. When you truly get that, you'll feel the confidence to step into your purpose, own your power, and make an impact in your own, unique way."

DO THIS TODAY: Try this challenge from Gabrielle: "Think about that today. Think right now about what makes you, you. When do you feel the most authentic and genuine?" #254Action

Day 110:
CT Fletcher

"My recovery was hard. I prayed to God. I told him, if this is going to be like this much longer, then just take me out. I don't want to live like this. I can't live like this. Just let me die. Because this is rough. But you know what? I didn't die, I kept living. A doctor came to me in the hospital. He said, 'I heard that you're a three-time world champion.' I said, 'Yes doctor, I am.' And he shook his head, it was a young doctor, he shook his head and said, 'Man, what happened to you?'

I want to thank that doctor for asking what happened to me. He asked me what happened to me with disdain in eyes. He couldn't believe that I had fallen that far. Because I looked like a human skeleton. He just couldn't believe it. He said, 'What happened to you?' You don't look like you ever lifted weight in your whole life.' But that doctor is what made me determined to get back out there. To climb back up to the top of the mountain and be king of the beasts once more. Thank you doctor. You made me do this."

DO THIS TODAY: Is there something you're passionate about that you've given up on? Can you pick it up where you left off and get back on track. #254Action

Day 110 High Five!

To give "110%" has become accepted language for giving more than one's maximum effort. Well, we're about to blow through 110 thanks to your dedication and hard work. Keep that effort going. High Five!

Day 111:
Eric Schmidt

"Usually in companies, there's a notion of a hierarchy, a set of objectives, quarterly plans. We had none of that. Our theory was that the leadership, in particular the bottoms of leadership, really should be empowered by what we were doing, and we'd see how far they get. We didn't have an 18-month strategy. We just kept iterating.

What I learned from this, is that fast iteration is the key. The most important thing to do, is every week build a new product, a new idea. Just keep pushing. You'd be amazed how much progress you make."

DO THIS TODAY: What's the one thing that you feel really good about right now? Do you have a product? A service? An art form? A skill? A talent? How good would it feel to take 10 minutes and consider how to make it better? Little by little, you can make transformative changes by pushing. #254Action

Day 112:
Kate Winslet

"When I was younger, when I was only 14, I was told by a drama teacher that I might do okay if I was happy to settle for the fat girl parts. Look at me now. Look at me now!

What I feel like saying in those moments is, to anyone who has ever been put down by a teacher or a friend or even a parent, just don't listen to any of it. Because that's what I did. I didn't listen and I kept on going, and I overcame all of my fears, and I got over a lot of insecurity, and just keep doing it. Keep believing in yourself, you know. That's what I felt like I really had to dig deep and do."

DO THIS TODAY: Did someone once say something to you that's holding you back? Are you even aware of it? Let what they said to you go and prove them wrong. Look forward to the day when you can say "Look at me now!" #254Action

Day 113:
John Lee Dumas

"Whenever people reach out to me and say, 'I'm doubting what I'm doing,' I say, 'Well congratulations, you're a human being. That's what it means to be a human.' You doubt what you do. It's that voice inside our head. It's innate in all of us. We're born with imposter syndrome. We don't walk outside of the cave at dark with a saber-toothed tiger outside. It's like there's a voice saying, 'Don't walk outside. It's dangerous.'

We don't live in that same world anymore, but we still have that inside our heads. We need to learn to not let it control our lives. To embrace that fear. I still have it every single day. I still wake up and say, 'Man should I be doing this webinar?' I have these doubts and these fears. And that's just the reality and I've just learned to embrace that."

DO THIS TODAY: Consider if your fears actually even come true. When you step out of your comfort zone, do your fears come true? When you doubt yourself, do negative things really happen? The truth is, those fears really don't come true that often, so next time you're feeling anxious or doubtful, remind yourself to trust in yourself. #254Action

Day 114:

Aaron Marino

"I would come to realize that the reason that I was put on this earth, is to help guys feel better about themselves. This passion and this desire to help burns so deeply inside of me, and I feel it through every ounce of my body and soul. Confidence is the key to feeling great about yourself. Without it you will absolutely never know your true potential or how amazingly powerful you could possibly be. So when I realized that it was confidence that I wanted to try and facilitate in other people, I told others about it. They said, 'You can't teach confidence. Either you have it or you don't.' And these were people that I respected, and it sort of got to me a little bit.

But I wanted to keep talking about things that I felt were important to develop character. Then something remarkable happened. I got an email from a guy who told me that through watching my videos he actually felt better about himself, and more confident. This was the best day of my life. And something else strange happened. I got another one, and another one. I realized that I was right. You absolutely can learn to be confident. The interesting thing about confidence, or any skill for that matter, is that you need to continually nurture and do the things that you did in order to get to that level of confidence. It's not a destination. It's a journey that you're going to be on your entire life."

DO THIS TODAY: Think of someone in your life who has helped you, at some point, to feel more confident. Send them a quick thank you message. If you can't think of anyone, message Aaron. #254Action

Day 115:
Warren Buffett

"You will move in the direction of the people that you associate with, so it's important to associate with people that are better than yourself. And actually the most important decision many of you will make will be the spouse you choose.

You really want to associate with people who are the kind of person you'd like to be. You'll move in that direction, and the most important person by far in that respect is your spouse. I can't overemphasize how important that is.

The friends you have, they will form you as you go through life. Make some good friends, keep them for the rest of your life, but have them be people that you admire as well as like."

DO THIS TODAY: Pick three people in your life, and write down three traits you admire most about them. What can you learn from them to become a better version of yourself? #254Action

Day 116:
Ralph Smart

"Stay calm. How we feel internally is how we carry ourselves externally. You can smile when you're dealing with people that you don't resonate with, difficult people. Keep calm, that inner balance is essential. Keep your head up.

A lot of people walk around their whole life with their head down to the ground. Keep your back straight. Stand your ground. You don't have to become confrontational with anybody, but we all must tap into our inner power, because the power is within. We have to really be connected to who we are. Breathe easy.

Once you can be calm, and not become so reactive, a lot of people that annoy us, they want us to fall into their trap. Difficult people, whether it's at work, wherever it may be, they want you to battle with them. Whatever you fight, you give energy to. Therefore, resistance makes you stronger. You can become silent. Say what you want to say, but once you become silent within yourself, you develop inner peace and balance. And therefore that difficult person is no longer difficult. There are no difficult people. It's how we interpret what is difficult. It is our interpretation of what it means to be difficult. It's different for every single person on the planet."

DO THIS TODAY: When people are difficult, remind yourself that it isn't usually about you. Don't feel doubt or blame when you don't know the reason behind their actions. Just move on with your day. #254Action

Day 117:
Judge Judy

"I remember doing a photo shoot my first year, right before we launched. And the marketing people were in Los Angeles, so this marketing guy sent his son, who was about 26 or 27, dressed the part, looked perfect. And he was sitting there and said to me, 'No, I don't think you should wear that, I think you should wear this color and I think you should move.' And I said to him, 'You know I have food in my refrigerator older than you are. And I've managed to get by, knowing what my good side is.' I mean, I'm not a glam person, so people aren't really interested in the glamorous side, the unglamorous side, they're just happy they get me vertical. If they get me vertical they should be happy.

So at age 52, coming into a new business, if you've had a good career, you come in with confidence. That's what it's all about. That's what business is all about, confidence. You know the song says you can be a hero or a zero. The difference is confidence. If you have created a portfolio for yourself, even in your own head, that you are really special and you know your business and nobody knows whatever part of that business that you do better than you do – that gives you confidence. I knew nobody knew more than I did about family court, and about judging. Nobody knew how to be a tactician in the court better than I did."

DO THIS TODAY: Write down three of your special talents or gifts. Now brainstorm how they might help you move your goals forward. #254Action

Day 118:

Brendon Burchard

"Have you ever struggled to be more disciplined? You've got that paper due next week but you don't do anything all week even though you know it's coming. Or you set up a brand new habit that you're so excited about that you know can improve your life, your relationships, or your work, but you don't stick to it. Or you started that workout routine and you got really pumped up, fired up and do it. You've lost a couple pounds, but then three weeks later it was gone, and what did you blame?

You blamed your discipline. You think, 'Ah, I wish I was more disciplined and everything would be great.' And the reality is, it's true. Discipline is one of the most important things we can develop in our lives because without that ability to be self-reliant and willful to get things done on a continual basis, we never get that great amount of momentum and progress towards what we really want. I bet there's a lot of areas of your life that could really benefit from being more disciplined. Whether you're eating healthier, or working out more often, or being more disciplined about doing your art, or contributing, or even being more disciplined about just speaking up for yourself when you know that you should."

DO THIS TODAY: Attack self-doubt through discipline. What are you stopping yourself out of fear or uncertainty from doing? Speak up for yourself, do it today, and make a practice of doing it consistently. #254Action

Day 119:

Evan Carmichael

"Just do what you love. This is cliché, but it's the number one rule in my book *Top 10 Rules for Success*. It's the most common thing that people say who've achieved massive success. You have to do the thing that you love. If you're doing work that you love, you're more likely to follow through, you're more likely to do it because it doesn't feel like work because you love doing it. I love thinking about my YouTube channel. I love thinking about Toronto Dance Salsa. I love thinking about the investments that I'm making in different companies. I love thinking about the big vision of where I'm going. I love doing it, so it's not work. It's not a chore.

If you wake up and you see this list of things that you have to do, and you just think, 'Man, this sucks, I can't wait for this day to be over.' If that's you, and that's most days, that's not a great life.

That means you need to change what you're doing, because you can only force yourself to do something that you don't like for so long before you give up and quit.

You will never achieve amazing success, you'll never be the best at what you do, you'll never be happy if you're constantly doing work that you hate. Because the people that love doing that work will destroy you. So better to eliminate that as soon as you can and move toward a path of doing work that you actually love."

DO THIS TODAY: Take one thing that you dread doing and find a way to get it off your schedule. Automate it. Delegate it. Or maybe even just eliminate it so you can focus on your energies on things that lift you up, instead of drain your soul. #254Action

Day 120:
Elliot Hulse

"People will come to me for advice on fitness, on building their businesses, their relationships, whatever the case may be. The place that they're dropping the ball is in bad habits, or not building productive habits. It's very difficult to just get up and change your life, just change the way you do things.

People like to say that all the time, 'Hey, just stop doing this', or, 'Start doing that.' They like to give advice, but the underlying factor is that whoever is asking the question is not disciplined enough to actually put that thing into action, get that thing done. The thing that I have always told my clients is, start with a small win. Begin with something small. For example, if you want to lose weight, I tell people, 'Just start walking every single morning. Don't worry about counting calories. Don't worry about complex workout ideas. Don't worry about anything that anyone is selling you. Just get up and walk every morning.

Now, it's not the walking that's actually going to make that person successful. It will add to your success, because getting up and walking, fresh air, and exercise is going to support you in losing weight. But, we all know there's far more factors to consider. What it will do, is create the virtue of discipline and commitment. They go together. When that small win, associated with getting up every single morning, is under your belt, you're going to feel the courage, the confidence, and you will have the ability to begin adding other things to grow stronger. Now it's been 60 days. 90 days, and it's like you've got that pattern down pat. You get up every morning and you just walk, that it. You don't think about it. It's become a habit.

You now can use that tool of creating habits, and instilling discipline with the next one, which should be a little bit more advanced. Perhaps only drink water with your meals. Don't

159

drink any soda, don't drink any juice, just drink water. That's the next one. And then the next one becomes more complex, and the next one becomes the more complex. Now, it might seem like this is tedious and slow, but I guarantee you that after 90 days of tiny wins, and the revamping of your character, you will be the type of person that can get anything done, at any time. And the long-time perspective is going to be a successful one for you.

Start small, have big wins with these little things, and then use that new version of yourself, that new character tool to attack bigger, and more advanced things, until you reach your goal."

DO THIS TODAY: If you're reading this book every day, congratulations! You've been building a small consistent habit. If not, commit to doing it. Each day only takes a minute or two to read but it will shape your confidence as well as your belief system that you can stay consistent on habits. #254Action

Day 121:
Lin-Manuel Miranda

"You push through it. You push through it because what's the alternative? You're going to leave that idea stuck in your head forever? That sucks. The alternative is you go through life and you had this great idea, and nothing came of it because you got tired.

Sometimes, you don't go to the party that all your friends are at because the idea is calling to you in that moment. 'Wait For It' is a great example of that. I was on my way to my friend's birthday party when that lyric showed up, when 'death doesn't discriminate' showed up in my head. I started writing it down on the train, the A train. Break dancers are dancing, I have my headphones on. I get out, the whole chorus comes, all at once. I write it down, and I suddenly see the shape of the whole song. I go into my friend's party. I go, 'Hey, what's up, man? Happy birthday, I have to go!' I get on the L train, and I write the rest of the song on the way back home, from the L to the A back up to 207th Street. You have to do that sometimes. You have to say no to your friends to say yes to your work, because what're you going to do? Lose that idea because you decided to have a drink with your friends? It's not worth it. Your friend will still be there!"

DO THIS TODAY: When inspiration strikes, commit to seeing your ideas through until you've fully worked them out in your head. That's the only way you'll see if they'll live up to their potential. #254Action

Day 122:
Usain Bolt

"I've seen different athletes over the years, when they train, they try to overdo it. You have to work with what the coach says. A lot of people, they run hard and harder and harder and then you can't finish a set.

One thing I've learned over the years from my coach is that the last one is the most important one. That's when you improve. So if you run, if you've got 16, you're in 5 and you're dying, you have to take a little bit more rest time. Take one more minute and go.

That's when you start improving. That's when the work pays off because your legs are dead and you have to push your body. You've got to overcome. It's like you're moving past a barrier, moving a step forward. A lot of people just want to stop cause they're dead tired. But you have to do the extra one."

DO THIS TODAY: Define what "going the extra mile" means for you when it comes to building your confidence. #254Action

Day 122 High Five!

Socio-economist Randall Bell found that those who read seven books or more per year are 122% more likely to be millionaires as opposed to those who never read or read one to three books. Reading this book is like reading a page from 254 different books. You're building your success one page at a time. High Five!

Day 123:
Arnold Schwarzenegger

"The body is very important, but the mind is more important than the body. You have to visualize what that body ought to look like in order to make it win. Because that's what creates the will. The will that you need to go to the gym every day. The will that makes you go into the forced reps. The will that makes you go beyond when you do your 500-pound reps in the squats and you can't do another rep and your body's shaking. It's the will that makes you go one more time down and struggle up one more time.

Since all of this mental aspect motivates you and that makes the difference between you being in the gym full of joy and looking forward to doing that extra rep and looking forward to doing those extra 100 reps in the sit-ups and working past the pain barriers, that's always the mind, it's not the body.

This is why I think the body is very important but the mind is more important than the body."

DO THIS TODAY: If you're struggling with self-discipline, list the temptations that may be distracting you from your goals. Look at that list today and tell yourself you're going to be greater than your temptations. #254Action

Day 124:
Robin Sharma

"Our weaker selves think that success in life is always being in the sunshine. Always being successful. Society has sold us a bill of goods that if we're not successful, and we're not on our games, and if we're not waking up happy, and if we're not full of joy, and if we're not feeling all this confidence, there is something that is wrong. That is just your ego screaming.

And that's why I say flow with the seasons. A life beautifully lived is a series of seasons. A legendary producer is not always at the top of the mountain. So, stop resisting the natural flow of epic performance. When you stop struggling, you learn to relax with life and you simply understand part of living a legendary business life, living a rare air personal life means you're going to have seasons of so-called success in society. Maybe it's making a lot of money, being really productive, being at the top of your game, receiving the accolades of peers, feeling you are nailing your goals and your ambitions. And you're going to have seasons where you're confused. Seasons where you feel heartbroken. Seasons where you feel depleted. Seasons where you are struggling. And the more you learn to relax into every season, the more you will generate this internal power which I call confidence."

DO THIS TODAY: View yourself as a work in progress. Look at the bigger picture and feel confident about everything you've achieved on your journey so far. #254Action

Day 125:
Bob Proctor

"I was reminded this morning, of a question I'm often asked: 'How do you eliminate fear from your life?' I don't think you ever do. I think you become courageous. Courageous people are not people without fear, courageous people are people that face the things they fear. There's no courage without fear. Whenever you go to do something that you've never done before, fear is going to step in. Now some people are afraid of flying. People are afraid of different things that can make them very, very uncomfortable.

I was afraid of flying. One day I was flying somewhere, and I wasn't very comfortable. I was sitting in the plane. There was a guy sitting beside me. He was very laid back, reading, one leg up over the other. Reading his newspaper. And we hit some rough weather. It got turbulent. That plane was bouncing all over the place. This guy's there holding his paper and he never skipped a breath. I was gripping on to the seats and he just kept reading. When the flight finally smoothed out, I looked over at him, and I hadn't even spoken to him up until that point. I said, 'Pardon me, how come you weren't scared back there?' He smiled, and he said, 'Well, I fly these things. In fact, I train people to fly these things.' I said, 'You know, I can't understand why this plane 'doesn't fall right out of the sky. I mean, why it doesn't go straight down.' He started to laugh, and said, 'You can fly a rock if you've got enough thrust behind it.' When he said that, I could see myself throwing a rock. And the rock was flying. You never think of a rock flying when you throw it. But the rock was flying. As long as there's thrust, the rock will fly.

Then I got to thinking, there's millions of pounds of thrust in these big engines. And you know something? I've never been uncomfortable since. If we're afraid of something, it's because we don't understand it. Fear is caused by ignorance of the unknown. But when you understand it, fear leaves.

Go study the principle of flight. See how the air is wrapped around the wings. It's wrapped around the wings, yet holds the plane up there. Don't permit fear to control your life. Absolutely refuse to. Someone said fear knocked on the door, faith opened it, and there was no one there.

You see, you eliminate fear through intelligent action. Face the thing you fear, and fear will leave you. I won't permit fear to control my life. Not even for five minutes. I used to let fear control me all the time. Almost all the time. Fear is caused by the unknown.

Think of the people that are afraid to go into their own business. They're afraid to move to the place they'd really like to go. They're afraid to ask the girl or the guy for a date. What are they doing? Their life is drying up, it's shrinking. We're only here for a short time. Make it a good time. Get rid of the fear. Face it."

DO THIS TODAY: Follow Bob's advice: "If there's something you're afraid of, go study it. Understand it. Talk to someone who's a professional in that particular area. But for goodness sake, don't let it control your life anymore." #254Action

Day 126:
Brian Tracy

"Another way to become a great conversationalist is to question for clarification. Never assume that you understand what the other person is saying or trying to say.

Instead, if you have any doubt at all, ask 'How do you mean?' Or, 'How do you mean exactly?' Then just pause and wait. This is the most powerful question I've ever learned for guiding and controlling a conversation. It's almost impossible not to answer this question.

When you ask, 'How do you mean?' The other person cannot stop himself or herself from answering more extensively. You can then follow up with other open-ended questions and keep the conversation rolling along."

DO THIS TODAY: Make an effort to ask someone today "How do you mean exactly?" before you automatically reply with your thoughts. #254Action

Day 127:
Evan Carmichael

"The first step in destroying self-doubt is understanding what you stand for, it's figuring out your One Word. That's why I wrote a book on it.

When you can understand what it is that you stand for, when you understand what you believe in then it's so much harder for someone to squash you down. People are just living a reactionary life, where when you understand that thing that really means the world to you, you start to live your life on your terms.

For me it's about #Believe. You can't crush me anymore because I know my path. I have certainty. When you have certainty you don't have the self-doubt. You don't worry when other people criticize you because you know the path that you're on.

I highly encourage all of you to figure out what it is that you stand for to create that certainty within yourself so that other people's opinions don't impact you, so that your own negative talk doesn't impact you."

DO THIS TODAY: Pay attention to your self-criticism or personal, self-doubting thoughts. For every discouraging thought you have today, come up with comebacks to shut your negative voice up. #254Action

Day 128:
Gabrielle Bernstein

"Witness fear. Be the nonjudgmental witness of it. Look at it and say, 'Something has to give.' If you're unwilling to look at your fear head-on, and honor it, and witness, I always say, 'If you don't show up for what's up it will keep showing up.' So looking and saying, 'I witness my resistance,' and you see that fear as resistance.

Fear is a resistance to what it is that you desire, and in the absence of resistance you become a magnet for what you desire. When you let go of that fear, and you transcend that fear, that's when you start to become a super-attractor. That's when you start to let what is truly of essence for you into your life, what is truly of service for you into your life, what is true happiness into your life. You open up your consciousness. You crack open your consciousness to find solutions rather than fight problems."

DO THIS TODAY: Follow Gabrielle's advice: "Look at the fear, witnessing it, calling it by its name, even if you don't have the tools yet. What happens is when you look at the fear and you think, 'Oh, I see this fear, I see this resistance. I see how it's blocking my life.' Then choose to see it differently." #254Action

Day 129:
Tony Hawk

"Fear is the best gauge of whether should you be in it or not. It's about approaching things with confidence. If I'm going to set out to do something, I've already convinced myself that I can do it. That it is possible. If I go at it and I think, I don't know if this is going to work. That's when I get hurt.

You can't just throw caution to the wind and go, 'Oh, let's see what happens.' Especially at my age and having this much experience and having so many injuries along the way, I'm way more methodical about learning things. It takes me way more tries and I have to know that it's going to work."

DO THIS TODAY: The right amount of fear helps you instead of hurting you. Use your fears constructively to question everything you do. Every time you felt doubtful today, write down ways you could have done things better so you're ready the next time it happens. #254Action

Day 130:

Gary Vaynerchuck

"I really think mindset is everything. You have to really decide are you going to be positive about things or negative? Am I thrilled that I have the ability to do things about it, to make what I'm worried about better? There are seven things I can fix tomorrow. I always choose positivity. I look at other people around me, it's not just about me. They choose positivity. I look at the people around me that are not winning, that are not progressing, that are not advancing, that are choosing negativity. It's stunningly binary. It's stunningly black and white. It's stunningly A or B.

This is really up to you. To be very honest, to be very frank, I think the biggest impact I'm having is shifting that mindset and making them understand that they're in charge. Hacking and trying to pour out the negativity, dump the negativity, add a positivity, dump a negativity, add a positivity, dump a negativity, add a positivity. I'm a positivity to your world. That's what I'm pushing, that's my agenda. I think you need to find more of that in your loved ones, in your business partner, in your audience."

DO THIS TODAY: Follow Gary's advice today. Dump a negative thought from your life and add a positive thought to your life. Try just one today. #254Action

Day 131:
Quentin Tarantino

"I grandiose my way out of fear. If I say I'm going to do one of the greatest car chases of all time, and if I don't, I'm not as talented as I thought I was. I will realize that there is a ceiling to my talent.

I said that to everybody. And was I scared? F yeah. I had trepidation going all the way because it's mine to fail. And it's failing in front of the mirror, too, because I'll know if I did it or not. I'll think, okay, you are not as good as you thought you were."

DO THIS TODAY: How can you grandiose your way out of fear with one of your goals today? #254Action

Day 132:
Brendon Burchard

"Begin with the end in mind. How do you want them to feel at the end of the conversation? What would you love them to think, believe, or do at the end? And what do you want to think, believe, or do at the end?

Always begin with that. People forget this all the time. They just have a spark of emotion or something they have to deliver and they just deliver it without knowing where to go, and if you don't where to go you end up in 50 different open alleys of conversation.

You open all these loops of conversation that don't get closed, people get confused, or you end up starting a fight that you didn't even know you are having, because you just weren't clear on where you wanted to go.

It doesn't mean you'll always get there exactly, because, again, humility says that you're going to learn together. But at least you'll have a sense of what feeling you want. Do you want her to trust you at the end of the conversation? Do you want him to know how you felt, and that's all you're after? What is it you really want at the end of the conversation?"

DO THIS TODAY: Plan a conversation with someone today and follow Brendon's suggestion. Think about how you want them to feel at the end of the conversation and try to make that happen. Then reflect. Did you actually make it happen? Where can you improve for next time? #254Action

Day 133:

Evan Carmichael

"Expect to suck at the start. A lot of times, when you're starting something, you know what looks good, and you want to be that good, but you can't be that good yet at the start because you're just starting out.

You might be starting on YouTube. And you look at somebody's videos, you might be looking at my videos, saying, 'I want to be like Evan.' Okay, that's a good goal. And your first video is going to suck. If I want to be like Les Brown, great, the first time I get on stage, I'm going to suck. Just expect to suck. No matter how much preparation, hard work, and energy and effort you put into it, you're going to suck the first time you do anything. And that's okay.

The next thing is, you do it again, you get better. Like anything else, any skill that you've learned, from the English language, or whatever language you speak, to whatever musical instrument you might play, to whatever sport you've picked up, the first time you tried that, you sucked. That's what always happens. And then with persistence and follow through, you get better. Don't let the self-doubt creep in."

DO THIS TODAY: Go out and suck at something today. Try something you were afraid of, expect zero results, and feel how great it is to know that you gave it a shot. #254Action

Day 133 High Five!

133 in mathematics is referred to as a "happy number." So let's be happy! You're 133 days in and still going. Keep that momentum happening. High Five!

Day 134:

Aaron Marino

"Eliminate negative people from your life. Negativity is more contagious than crabs. When you surround yourself or have negative little cancerous people in your life, they directly impact your confidence in a negative way.

Negative nasty people. Nasty. Not like good nasty, bad nasty. As in, 'Get the freak away from me I want nothing to do with you.'

Now here's the issue when I say, 'Hey, just get rid of negative people.' It's like, poof, they're gone, right? Wrong Because a lot of times we have these negative people or these energy vampires all around us.

They might be at work, they might be at school, they might actually even be related to us. Does this mean that you may need to find a new job? Yeah. Maybe a new relationship? Quite possibly. Is it going to suck for a little while now? Yes. In the long run is it going to pay off big-time in terms of your confidence? Yes!"

DO THIS TODAY: Who is the biggest energy vampire in your life? How can you stop being around them or limit how much time you spend with them? #254Action

Day 135:
Gaur Gopal Das

"I want to discover my own mold. I want to have a paradigm that I have invented. Only when you discover yourself, when you live a life that you were created for, will you feel happy and satisfied. You'll also be super effective.

In the corporate world today, loads of people are just living a life which they're not created for, because it pays the big bucks. And why do they need the bucks? To pay their taxes, to pay the bills, to pay the mortgages. But they are not living a life of what they're created for. So it's basically fitting in, just because it pays you.

I decided I didn't want to fit in. So when I saw others moving on, my friends, my colleagues, moving on, higher, I really did not feel insecure at all, because I didn't want to fit in, to be someone else. I wanted to find myself, discover myself."

DO THIS TODAY: Make a choice today. Do you want to fit in with everyone else or live your own life? If you decided that you don't want to fit in then you also shouldn't care what everyone else has or is doing. Go be different. #254Action

Day 136:

John Addison

"Your habits determine what direction you're going in. Your success in life, are in direct proportion to your habits. What you do, not what you say you're going to do, but what are you going to do? You have to develop successful habits, and that starts with being a daily goal setter and a daily goal hitter. People spend their whole lives dreaming, but they're really just pipe dreams. They're thinking about what they want to be doing in 20 years. The future you need to be worried about is not the next 20 years, but the next 20 minutes. What are you going to be doing to be effective?

When you get up every day, know your priorities. Life will overwhelm you. Stuff will overwhelm you. It's so easy to get consumed by a bunch of stuff that is not going to get you where you want to be. You have to choose to be effective. Know what your priorities are. Don't let your phone, don't let your tablet, don't let the TV, don't let your friends knock you off what are the most important things to get done today. Say, 'Every day, I will do today what others don't, so I will have tomorrow what others won't.' Make today your masterpiece. Get up today and get stuff done. Finish the day. Attack the day, and go change your life."

DO THIS TODAY: What's the most important thing that you need to do in the next 20 minutes? Think about it. Then go actually do it. #254Action

Day 137:
Sheryl Sandberg

"How do you communicate authentically? How do you figure out what to say and what not to say in a way that's authentic? If you walk in the room, and this gets worse as you get more senior, and say, 'Here's the answer,' you're not giving anyone else any room to say anything.

It starts from the fundamental understanding that there is no truth. There's my truth, there's your truth, and everything is subjective. And so if you always start from the position of, 'This is what I believe, I don't expect you to believe it, I don't think you have to believe it, I'm not saying it's true,' you can actually always communicate authentically."

DO THIS TODAY: Try this tip from Sheryl next time you're in a meeting: "If you walk in the room and say, 'I believe this, for this reason, what do you believe?' If you share your truth in that language, you give people room to communicate authentically, that is hugely important to these relationships at any stage." #254Action

Day 138:
Sam Altman

"If you don't actually believe what you're doing, it's really important. If you don't derive satisfaction from what you're doing, then you will not be able to sustain all of the bad things that happen in the incredibly long period of time that the bad things happen over.

So the only motivation that I have seen work for people over a long period of time is enjoyment in what they're doing and an intense belief that it matters, and ideally liking the people that they go to work with every day.

It's totally cool when people start off saying, 'Well I want to make money, or, 'I want to be famous.' I think a lot of people start that way and they don't like to admit it, but pretty quickly, or at least in the first few years, I think a lot of people find a deeper mission for why they do what they do, and that that drives them then for the rest of the time they work."

DO THIS TODAY: Remember that building confidence in yourself and finding your passion can be a process of trial-and-error. If you want to start believing in yourself and your work, think about what things that are most important to you. What keeps you up at night? What could you obsess over? What would you enjoy doing enough that you can handle all the unpleasant parts? If you have more than one answer, make sure you're trying all these things out. #254Action

Day 139:
Nick Cannon

"Be the best you, you can possibly be and offer up what only you can offer up.

People may mistake it for arrogance or conceit. No, that's not what we are talking about here. We are talking about straight confidence.

Just sitting up straight, walking in a room, owning a room, demanding attention. That's what it is all about."

DO THIS TODAY: Today, you're going to perform a task with confidence, even if you feel self-conscious doing it. It's okay to feel foolish. Embracing embarrassment is part of the journey towards accomplishing something great. #254Action

Day 140:
Robin Sharma

"If you want to be more inspired, one of my favorite protocols is the daily nature walk. I love walking in the woods. I listen to audiobooks. I call it, reading while walking. I go to this place, it's sort of my creative forest. There's not a lot of people in there and I walk for one hour. I breathe in the air. I look at the lush scenery. I listen to a different audiobook. It's almost like walking meditation as well. Sometimes I don't listen to an audiobook and I just walk. And I touch the earth. It's almost like I'm thanking the earth, connecting with the soil. Yes I'm wearing shoes, I don't want to get too esoteric here but there's a lot of really good research saying, if you want to boost your immune system, you want to boost your happiness, you want to release serotonin and dopamine, you want to release the fear hormone called cortisol, walk in nature. If there's something I'm confused about, I just talk it out. I talk out loud trying to work it out. If I'm in pain I get the negative energy out of my system by just releasing it, by talking about it. I also do a walking blessing meditation. While walking, I challenge myself to come up with 50 things I'm grateful for. I verbalize those because it's only me and the squirrels in the woods. I say, 'I'm grateful for my family, my health, for work that feeds my soul, the sunset I watched last night, my team, my business, the travels that I get to take, the people that I serve.' It's an incredible protocol to install."

DO THIS TODAY: Go for a walk outside and come up with 50 things you're grateful for. #254Action

Day 141:

Brian Tracy

"Paraphrase the speaker's words in your own words. So after you have nodded and smiled you can then say, 'Well let me see if I've got this right,' or, 'Let me see if I understand you exactly. What you're saying is this,' and then you repeat it back in your own words.

By paraphrasing the speaker's words you demonstrate, in no uncertain terms, that you are genuinely paying attention and making every effort to understand his or her thoughts or feelings.

And the wonderful thing is when you practice effective listening other people will begin to find you fascinating. They will want to be around you. They will feel relaxed and happy in your presence because when you listen to other people you make them feel important."

DO THIS TODAY: Try Brian's method today. In your next conversation practice listening and then say, 'Let me see if I understand you exactly. What you're saying is...' #254Action

Day 142:
Jessie J

"If you want to be a fireman, go and do it. If you want to be a ballet dancer, then go and be a ballet dancer. If you don't believe in yourself, then no one else will believe in you.

It's so important for me to be an inspiration. I was bullied, as nine out of 10 children are, and I wanted to be a role model. I think now I'm in the limelight to go, 'It's okay.'

It's the special people that are bullied. The ones that have something magical. It's something that you can turn into a positive and not let it eat you away.

There'll always be someone that says, 'You can't do it.' There'll always be someone that says, 'I don't believe in you.' There'll always be someone that says, 'I do believe in you.' And there's always someone that says, 'You can do it.'

That's the people that you have to focus on. However much people try and put me down, which they do, they say, 'Every time I hear your song I want to burn my ears.' I say, 'Who's laughing now?'"

DO THIS TODAY: Remind yourself that it's the special people that are picked on. You have something magical. Now turn that into a positive. #254Action

Day 143:
Mel Robbins

"It all comes down to one word. You know what I'm talking about? The F-bomb. It's everywhere. You hear it all the time, and I honestly don't understand what the appeal is of the word. I mean, you don't sound smart when you say it. And it's really not expressing how you really feel. It's sort of a cheap shot to take.

Of course, you know I'm talking about the word: 'fine.' 'How you doing?' 'Oh I'm fine.' Oh really, you are? Dragging around those extra 40 pounds, you're fine? Feeling like roommates with your spouse, and you're fine? Really? I don't think so. But, see here's the deal with saying that you're fine. It's actually genius.

Because if you're fine, you don't have to do anything about it. When you think about this word, fine, it just makes me so angry. I mean, here we are at a conference about being alive and you're going to describe the experience of being alive as 'fine?'

What a flimsy and feeble word. If you're crappy, say you're crappy. If you're amazing, say you're amazing. Tell the truth. Oh, 'I don't want to burden you with the fact that I hate my life.' Or 'Hey, I'm amazing,' but that would make you feel terrible.

The bigger issue with 'fine' is that you say it to yourself. That thing that you want, I guarantee you, you've convinced yourself that you're fine not having it. That's why you're not pushing yourself.

It's the areas in your life where you've given up. Where you've said, oh I'm fine. My mom's never going to change, so I just can't have that conversation. I'm fine, we have to wait until the kids graduate before we get divorced, so we'll just sleep in separate bedrooms. I'm fine. I lost my job, I can barely pay my bills, but whatever, it's hard to get a job.

One of the reasons why this word also just annoys me so much is that scientists have calculated the odds of you being born. The odds of you being born at the moment in time you were born, to the parents you were born to, with the DNA structure that you have? One in 400 trillion! Isn't that amazing?

You're not fine, you're fantastic! You have life changing ideas for a reason, and it's not to torture yourself. All day long you have ideas that could change your life, that could change the world, that could change the way that you feel, and what do you do with them? Nothing."

DO THIS TODAY: The next time someone asks you how you're doing don't reply with 'I'm fine.' Pause, reflect to think about how you actually are, and give an honest answer. #254Action

Day 144:
Usain Bolt

"When you go in the race, you have to go in there always confident.

You can't go in there thinking, 'The guy next to me is going to beat me today.' Even if you know he's going to beat you, you have to be confident. That 'I'll give him a run for his money today. I'll give my best.' You can't worry about anybody else. Because he may come out and have a really bad day.

And then what? See? You have to be ready just in case he has a bad day. You have to be on your game at all times."

DO THIS TODAY: Next time you catch yourself comparing yourself to someone else, snap out of it. Your goal today is to focus on doing the best you can do and being proud of the effort you put in. #254Action

Day 145:

Gary Kasparov

"Alexander Bell, the inventor of the telephone, had a stack of notebooks where he recorded every failed experiment. So, if you look really hard you can find the winning spot, even in the midst of your numerous failures.

The ex-speaker of U.S. House of Representatives, Newt Gingrich, hit the right points when he said that perseverance is hard work you do after you get tired of doing the hard work you already did."

DO THIS TODAY: Have something you need to have more perseverance in? Create a calendar and mark an X every time you do it. Feel the power, momentum, and confidence every time you mark an X on the calendar. Celebrate your success regularly. #254Action

Day 146:
Priyanka Chopra

"Quantico was my first audition. I knew I had to go into this room and read these lines in front of all these people, but I was so nervous before I went in. So, I went to the bathroom before, and I looked in the mirror, and it's so stupid and cliché, but I talked to myself, and I said, 'What's wrong with you? You've played the most difficult characters in the most complicated movies.' I tossed my hair a little bit, felt great, and walked out. Did my bit, and I got the job."

DO THIS TODAY: Today, you're going to give yourself a pep talk in the mirror, no matter how silly you feel doing it. So go right now and make it happen! #254Action

Day 147:

Tim Ferriss

"'How do you define risk?' This is an important question, because I realized that a lot of the knots we tie ourselves into, and a lot of the anxiety that we feel, is actually due to using words that are not defined very well.

Like 'success.' 'I just want to be successful.' Well you better have a very clear definition of what that is if it's going to be one of your main obsessions. 'Happiness.' Ooh, that's a slippery one too.

And 'risk' is another one. Risk, to me, is the likelihood of an irreversible negative outcome. So defined that way, there are actually very few serious risks. And I choose to take very few serious risks. People might view me as a risk-taker. I don't view myself that way at all."

DO THIS TODAY: What do the words success, happiness, and risk mean to you? #254Action

Day 148:
Eric Thomas

"When I've been telling you to get that goal, what I've been talking about is consistency. And for some of you, for real, you'll never have it. You'll never be it. You'll never do it, because you don't have any consistency. Listen to me, you are killing me and killing yourself.

You start and you stop, and then you start, and you stop. We're talking about the power of 21. I'm talking about doing something for 21 straight days. Now, it may not work. I remember when I first did this. The first thing I started with my boy. He gave me a book called the book of Proverbs, and he told me to read a book of Proverbs a day for 21 days. He said 'E, just start a habit.'

We started with reading Proverbs, something real simple. But he said 'E, if you can do something for 21 days, you'll never have to think about it.'

I woke up at three o'clock this morning. Three o'clock, burnt out, tired. And I just went back to sleep. Three minutes later, my body woke me up.

What am I saying to you? I'm telling you consistency, matters. My body's saying 'Yo, E, I don't know what you're doing. I don't know what you think you're doing, but we don't do that. Sleep is for suckers. Get up!' My body kicked in and said, 'Get up!' We're talking about consistency.

And so, I read the book of Proverbs, 21 straight days. Then I started doing other stuff. Like exercise for 21 straight days. I just started trying to do stuff for 21 days, to see if I could do it. And I'm going to be honest with ya'll. I did 14 days, then I started all over again.

Next time I did 16 days, then I started all over again. Then I did 18 days, and I started all over again. Then I did 21. Some stuff I can do 21 straight days. Some stuff I have to start and stop, but when you get to 21, there's power in consistency."

DO THIS TODAY: For this process of gaining confidence to work you need to be consistent. You're on Day 148 but have you been taking days off? You are cheating yourself. For the next 21 days and then until the end, stay consistent. Your future, more confident self will thank you. Let's go! #254Action

Day 148 High Five!

148 is Dunbar's number. It's a suggested limit to the number of people you can keep stable social relationships with. You might be limited by how many people you can stay friends with, but there's no limit to the knowledge you can digest. It's time to blow past 148. High Five!

Day 149:
Dr. Ivan Joseph

"The easiest way to build self-confidence? There's no magic button. Repetition, Repetition, Repetition. What does Malcolm Gladwell call it? The 10,000 hour rule?

There's no magic button. I recruited a goalie from Colombia, South America, one year. Big, tall six-foot-three man. He had hands like stone. I thought he was like Flipper. Every time I'd throw him the ball... down, down onto the ground. He said, 'Oh my God, we're in trouble.'

Simple solution? Get to the wall, kick a ball against the wall, and catch it. Kick the ball against the wall, and catch it. His goal was 350 a day, for eight months. He came back, his hands were calloused, the moisture on his hands were literally gone. He is now playing in Europe. Was it magic? No. Repetition, repetition, repetition. The problem is, we expect to be self-confident, but we can't be, unless the task we're doing is not novel, is not new to us. We want to be in a situation where we've had so much pressure. Because pressure builds diamonds.

We want to be in a situation where you can say, 'Hey, I've done this 1,000 times.' I did my speech, I practiced in from of the mirror. Thought, 'Hey, I'm sounding good,' and then I went in front of my kids and my wife, I was like, 'Oh, gosh, got a little nervous.' Then I get in front of Glen Gould. 'Oh my goodness, I'm a little more nervous.' By the time I get to the ACG, where 2,500 people are there, I won't have a single ounce of nervousness, because of my ability to practice, over and over and over again.

The problem with repetition is, how many of us bail after the first bit of failure? How many of us bail after the first bit of adversity? Depends who you ask, Edison took anywhere from 1,000 to 10,000 tries to build that light bulb. Do you know how many publishers J.K. Rowling took her *Harry Potter* book to? I believe the number was 12 or 13. I'm pretty confident, but after two or three 'no's', I'd be thinking, 'Dang it.' After six or seven, I'd say, 'Maybe not.' Definitely after nine or 10, I'd be looking to be something else besides an author. Maybe it shouldn't be repetition, maybe the answer should be persistence, because we all repeat something, but very few of us really will persist.

So that's one way to build self-confidence. Get out there, do what you want to do and do not accept 'no' for an answer."

DO THIS TODAY: Think about one thing you're really good at because you've done it so many times. Now think about something you want to accomplish but you don't think you're good enough. You know what's about to come next don't you? Consider what it's going to take for you to be able to gain experience through repetition for the thing that you want to accomplish. Schedule the time. Gather the resources. Today you're going to start! #254Action

Day 150:
Chris Pratt

"I graduated high school and I moved out and became a door-to-door salesman. I was selling lower-priced items. Coupons for businesses in the service industry. I'd walk around and say, 'Hi, I'm from Meineke. Here you go, four oil changes, $20. Pretty great, right? Cash, check, or credit card today? And we'll take that fr-' 'No? Okay. F*** you, too, sir. Please don't sic your dog on me, I'm leaving.' I did the job for about a year and a half. And eventually I got asked to run the office in Colorado. But, failed miserably. They put a lien on my minivan. Pretty bad.

But backing up to answer how I got into stand-up comedy, there was a really high turnover rate in Seattle. One or two new guys a week would end up quitting by the end of the week. A lot of the money that you made is just from them selling three or four and them leaving. Because it's just the worst effing job anybody's ever effing done. It's great prep for being an actor in terms of lying, walking into a room feeling comfortable and having thick skin. There's no better. So you can tell me I'm as fat as you want, you can tell me anything you want, and it's not going to hurt my feelings. I've got really thick skin from being a door-to-door salesman."

DO THIS TODAY: Practice being rejected. Tell yourself it isn't personal. Make it a numbers game. Know for however many times you get rejected, you are bound to get a yes eventually. Do something today you expect to get rejected for to build your thicker skin and confidence. #254Action

Day 151:
Zendaya

"I would say if you truly believe in something and you really have a passion for something, then go for it. I think there's a lot of obstacles that you have to go through. And nothing's ever given to you. And it takes a lot of hard work and dedication, but if you really believe in it, then you should do it."

DO THIS TODAY: Make three lists. Under 'List 1' write down your strongest abilities. Under 'List 2' write down the areas or things you find most interesting. For those first two lists, find the overlaps and write them under 'List 3'. What thing on that list jumps out at you? Do you believe in it? Can you visualize yourself doing It? #254Action

Day 152:
Evan Carmichael

"It's so easy to get lost in your current situation. It's so easy to get lost in the present moment and that prevents us from making smart decisions. To be stuck, and to only look at the trees stops us from being able to take a step up and see the forest. To see a much bigger picture.

Your current world will change so many times. You will have many opportunities to reinvent yourself over the course of your life. It's easy to get lost in what your current short-term view of the world is and your life is, but you've got to have that extra perspective to think, 'I'm going to have multiple careers over my life.' It's not like you make one decision here today and that's for life. Make the decision. If it doesn't work out, you'll adjust.

The lesson is when you find that thing, you have to do it. So when you have that idea, when you have that spark, and you want to try to do something, instead of just sitting on the sidelines and being that person, do something! And if it doesn't work out, it's okay, because you'll have multiple opportunities in the future to continue to reinvent yourself. This one idea is not your forever idea. So just give it a shot and see if it works out."

DO THIS TODAY: Start dedicating time to that awesome thing you identified in yesterday's challenge. Recognize that you're not committing to it forever, just trying something for now. #254Action

Day 153:
Brian Tracy

"Visualize yourself performing or behaving in a particular way, in a particular situation. The more often you visualize and imagine yourself acting as if you already had the new habit, the more rapidly this new habit will be accepted by your sub-conscious mind, and eventually become automatic, like programming a computer."

DO THIS TODAY: For the next thing you want to achieve, visualize yourself doing it, and write down your visualization as a prompt on a piece of paper. Read it to yourself daily while you build the confidence to achieve it. #254Action

Day 154:
Drew Canole

"Change your physiology. I'm talking about your posture. I'm talking about your head up. I'm talking about head straight, maintain eye contact. That automatically sends a signal to you to be more confident. Try it out.

If you're slouching in your chair right now, if you're sitting on your couch, take a moment, sit up. Take a big breath. Breathing helps a lot as well. You have 80,000 messages that transfer up your spinal cord, into your limbic system, into your brain, that sends signals to your prefrontal cortex. They allow you to make effective decisions. Now that's a miracle of machine. The problem is, most people are hunched over, working at their computer all day. They're not moving enough. Then they sit in a car, they come home, they're watching TV again. It's ridiculous.

Elevate your posture, my friend. Lift it up. Maintain eye contact. Put your head back. Roll your shoulders back, and allow those signals to enter your brain so that you can make effective decisions and overall feel more confident. Because how you feel dictates who you are. It's all energy. It's all vibration in your emotion."

DO THIS TODAY: Set an alarm on your phone to go off every 30 minutes, and check your posture. Fix your slouch, sit up straight, and roll your shoulders back. Repeat until it becomes a habit. #254Action

Day 154 High Five!

Shakespeare famously wrote 154 sonnets and published them in a single quarto. You're 154 days in and with the growth you're getting, you'll be making a name for yourself soon enough as well. High Five!

Day 155:
Brendon Burchard

"Part of taking a risk is being more personal. Teaching yourself to share more, to be more vulnerable. It's hard, I get it. For my next level, I'm going to have to share more about my personal life. Be more thoughtful about that. It takes a lot of vulnerability. The first time I ever really shared with my audience, I shared that when I started my career, I went broke. I was struggling to start my career, do my own seminars. I had no idea what I was doing. People were making fun of me. It was new and it was scary. But I'll never forget that after I shared that, so many people would come up to me share their stories with me and it was really inspiring. And it taught me that people won't believe your successes if they don't believe the struggle.

You have to share where you struggled more in life and that feels like a risk but you have to be honest. Do your family and your friends and the people you serve know what you really desire in life? What you're really going after? What you need? Because if they don't know that about you, that's not taking risks. Being quiet and avoiding difficult conversation is not taking risks and it's not the path to growth. The path to growth for so many of us is another level of personal authenticity. And if you don't do that, then you're not risking, you're just going through the motions."

DO THIS TODAY: Deepen your connection with someone by sharing something personal, like the fact that you're reading this book! #254Action

Day 156:
Brian Tracy

"Take a deep breath. Be patient. Calm down. Go slow. Don't let other people's negativity, or anger, or frustration, affect you. There's a saying, 'If you can't say something nice don't say anything at all.' Sometimes the very best thing you can do in dealing with difficult people, is just to be dead silent. Don't feed the fire by arguing or getting involved. When you're dealing with a difficult person just stop the clock like a time out. Just smile and don't say anything. Then when you do say something, remember one of the great communication tools is this: The person who asks questions has control.

The way that you can take control of any negative situation is not trying to win, but simply by asking questions. Say, 'Why do you say that?' Or, 'Why do you feel that way?' Or, 'That's an interesting point of view. How did you come to that point of view? How would we know that what you say is true? Is there any proof or validity?' It's sort of like the matador backs away from the bull. As you keep backing away from the bull, you cape the difficult person by simply asking questions and being genuinely curious about what he or she is thinking and feeling and why they are behaving the way they are. Sometimes you may find that they have a good reason, or that they misunderstand something. Maybe you will find that they have a difficult problem in their lives. But it any case, be calm, be patient, be controlled, and ask questions."

DO THIS TODAY: Use this questioning tactic next time you're in a difficult situation. You're now armed with a powerful tool instead of feeling powerless around difficult people. #254Action

Day 157:
Brendon Burchard

"High performers have more energy. A high-performing athlete has more energy than one who's dogging it. We know that. There's a physical vitality. A mental stamina too, that goes along with their days.

The energy, it's just palpable. You can feel it around them. And of course, it's not luck. They're generating that energy. They're conditioning that energy in their body by their training regime. They're conditioning the energy in their mental stamina by having the clarity of what to focus on. What not to focus on. And getting very disciplined about where they give their time, energy, effort, attention.

So, they're not pulled in a million different places. Because you know how it is, if you're pulled in a million different places, or you're multi-tasking dozens and dozens of things, your energy is dissipated. Theirs is extraordinarily focused and powered up with reserves."

DO THIS TODAY: Focus your efforts by doing one thing at a time today. No distractions. No interruptions. No trying to multi-task. Try it for one day and see how much progress you can make on your goals. #254Action

Day 158:

Tim Ferriss

"You have to schedule, if you are a creator, blocks of time that are at least two to four hours or more in length. No Frankenstein's monster of twenty-minute breaks and ten-minute breaks combined into three hours will have the value of an uninterrupted block of three hours. If you are trying to make high-level decisions, focus on time-consuming, high-priority projects, push something to a next milestone as a maker, creator.

Point number two, you want to make sure you're producing the right things. You could make a ton of decisions. Check a lot of emails. Make a ton of phone calls. And at the end of the day, week, quarter, year, you've not accomplished all that much at all. The way that I get around that is looking at my list of goals, looking at my list of to-dos, and asking myself which of these, if done, would make all of the other ones easier or unnecessary?

This is a great way to narrow your focus to the most important domino that, when flipped over, will then topple 20, 30, 40 others. One thing I keep in mind a lot is this quote from Steve Jobs: 'Innovation is saying no to a thousand things.' And really, if you want to do anything impressive, anything incredible, you have to say no to 99% of what comes at you. If you don't have time, you don't have priorities, that's it."

DO THIS TODAY: Schedule a three-hour block today. Turn off your email. Do not pick up the phone. Do not let anyone bother you. Then once you've done that three-hour block, consider how much you accomplished and whether being offline for three hours really hurt your contacts and those trying to get a hold of you. #254Action

Day 159:

Brendon Burchard

"Decide you need no reason whatsoever to be more confident. Just make the decision to be confident. You don't need a reason. You don't need 50 people to tell you you're amazing or you're beautiful.

You just have to say, 'Today, I'm going to lift my head up a little bit. Today I'm just going to be confident. I'm going to walk into this room, I'm going to stand tall, as if I was an incredibly confident person for no other reason than that's my intention right now.'

That's it. That's the power of intention. It's the power of the human being that we get to choose how we want to feel. You could be happy right now for no reason. You don't need 50 things to make you happy. Just sense the moment, feel grateful for life. You're good to go. We over-complicate these things. We think we have to have some big, long story to suddenly one day wake up and be more confident. No, we don't.

Have you ever had a day where you just crushed it? You know, you got so much done, at the end of the day you thought 'Man, I just crushed it today.' That happened because when you woke up in the morning, you said, 'I'm going to get some stuff done today.' You had the intention to be a productive human being that day. So why not set the intention to be a confident human being that day?

You don't need a bunch of stuff. People really get this one wrong. And what happens is within the vacuum of intention arises impulse. And often from that impulse up comes worry, concern, fear. So we have to have the intention of who we are and what we're going to be.

Confidence doesn't have to mean you're leaping over tall buildings. Confidence means you're being who you are, authentically, for no other reason.

No one gave you permission. You just decided to be who you are. You decided to chase your dreams. That's confidence, right? Believing in yourself, and believing in where you're going, that's confidence. It doesn't take a whole lot of magic. That's confidence."

DO THIS TODAY: Make confidence an intention you set for today. Just decide that you will be confident today and see how that mindset shifts your day. #254Action

Day 160:
Amy Schumer

"I think having confidence is a lifelong battle. You'll feel like you're in a good place and then somebody makes a comment and you've got to pick yourself back up. I feel like I'm in a really good place with confidence, but I still have days where I feel like hot garbage.

I have moments where my confidence has definitely been too inflated and then also moments where I feel really invisible and bad about myself, too. I don't try to rush out of that space. I let myself be there for a minute and I think this is just a feeling, it'll be replaced by another feeling, and this is not my new reality, this is just a moment in time. I have a pretty good baseline. It's kind of hard to F with it at this point."

DO THIS TODAY: How confident are you feeling right now? Are you too inflated or do you feel invisible? Be there for a minute just to feel it and then replace it with a feeling of confidence that serves you better. #254Action

Day 161:

Tony Robbins

"I interviewed these 50 unbelievable investors. People that are macro traders. People like Warren Buffett, value people. Blood-in-the-streets type of people. You buy when the world is going to hell. They're all different, but they have four things in common. Number one, every single one of them was obsessed with not losing money. Guys like you and I tend to say how do we make money for our companies, for ourselves as an investor? Their entire focus is not losing money because they know if you lose 50% it takes 100% to get even.

These guys are obsessed with not being comfortable with risk. They don't want to take risks but the second key that they do is they're always focused on asymmetrical risk-reward. Most people think the most successful investors take huge risks to get huge rewards. And in reality, they take the least risk humanly possible to get the largest reward. Their whole focus is, how do I get a three to one or a five to one? If I risk trying to make five and I'm wrong, I'm risking that, I could be wrong four times and break even. So they have a completely different approach. They're all very focused, thirdly, on tax efficiency, because you only have the money you get to keep. And fourthly, it's all diversification. And those four things, fundamentally, are the frame from which you start to design a portfolio."

DO THIS TODAY: What's a five to one risk you can take today? Something that if you tried five times you would just need it to work out once to get to break even. #254Action

Day 162:
Gaur Gopal Das

"Whether you drive a Volkswagen or you drive a Bentley, the road remains the same doesn't it? Whether you make a call on a Samsung or an iPhone X, whoever you are calling remains the same doesn't it? Whether you're flying economy or you're flying business class, the destination where you are heading remains the same, doesn't it? Whether you are wearing a simple Fastrack or an Omega or a Rolex, the time remains the same, doesn't it?

It's quite amazing how we work ourselves up so much with increasing our standard of living that we forget to increase the standard of our life. Please do not compromise the standard of your life. That's what makes you happy. Very often, we forget to give attention to those things that can truly make us happy. Never ever, compromise on those principles. If all you have is money, you are the poorest person in the world. There is way more to life than what money can buy. If you truly want to know how rich you are, drop a tear and see how many hands come to wipe that tear. Our happiness and our increased standard of life are not in things, it's in people. It's relationships, it's meaningful, deep bonds of love that bring fulfillment to the heart. It's those meaningful exchanges of love that we share with each other in relationships, that brings true joy.

Isn't it the greatest irony, that something that brings the greatest fulfillment, we very conveniently neglect in just running after increasing and enhancing our standards of living?"

DO THIS TODAY: What's a change you can make today that will increase the standard of your life, not just your standard of living? What meaningful conversation can you have with someone today to bring them and you more joy? #254Action

Day 162 High Five!

162 is the total number of baseball games each team plays during a regular season in Major League Baseball. It's more than football, hockey, or basketball. It's a marathon. You're passing 162 now. Continue to be an example of consistency and your goals will soon become within your reach. High Five!

Day 163:
Paul McGee

"Some people wear negativity like an old comfortable coat. It just seems to fit them really well. They're the kind of people that, even if they won the lottery would say, 'Just my luck, it wasn't the Rollover week.' You know what their mantra for life is? 'Never forget, every silver lining has a black cloud.'

I want us to be careful of these people because sometimes I think we need to challenge them. I think they're unaware of how their negativity and their misery can impact those around them. Maybe you could even use humor to diffuse the situation. You know, 'How long have you been a motivational speaker then?' Although people might be miserable by nature, let's be prepared to challenge that."

DO THIS TODAY: What negative phrases do you find yourself saying regularly? The next time you catch yourself saying it, what will you replace it with? Who can you ask around you to help you catch it as well? #254Action

Day 164:
CT Fletcher

"Confidence is the key to so many things. But it's mistaken for arrogance. For Muhammad Ali, probably my only idol as a kid, he was so confident in his ability it was mistaken as arrogance. But he was so sure, so confident he could not be beaten. I have experienced that type of confidence. When I walked into a competition, I would ask, 'Which one of you mothers is coming in second?' I meant that s***. I was totally, totally confident that whoever the F showed up was coming in second. How do you develop that type of confidence? Through obsession. You have to be obsessed with whatever you're trying to obtain. In order to develop that, you're obsessed with tiddlywinks, you're obsessed with hopscotch, obsessed with pulling teeth, obsessed with trimming hedges, washing dishes, whatever the F you do. If you want to be thoroughly confident in it, you must become obsessed with it. Powerlifting was my passion, my obsession, and I developed through hard-a** work. I knew without a shadow of doubt that that next mother had not worked as hard as I had worked. I couldn't be maxing out my desire, my want, my drive, my will. In those areas, I could not be touched. There wasn't a human on the effing planet who could match me on those areas, so having that total confidence in my ability, there was no way I could lose. I convinced myself that I was invincible. Convince yourself that you cannot lose. Convince yourself that you are the best. Convince yourself that nobody can outwill you, nobody can out-want you. Convince yourself of those things and you will have effing confidence. Convince yourself that you can't be stopped."

DO THIS TODAY: That thing that you want to be more confident in, make it your obsession today. Spend part of the day learning. Watch videos, read articles, listen to a podcast. Then the rest of the day practicing, practicing, practicing. As you get better, your confidence will soar. #254Action

Day 165:
Tom Bilyeu

"There's a gap between who people are and what they tell you they want to accomplish. In the beginning, I hired everyone, everyone. Not because I'm super smart and thought I should. There was no one else! I did the interviews and I realized that these guys tell me they want to do something amazing with their life, and then I realize they can't execute on that dream. They don't have the mindset yet.

In her amazing book Mindset, Carol Dweck says some people believe they're as smart as they're ever going to be, and they're going to be ego protective and they're going to try to thwart anything that makes them feel like they're not the smartest person.

Then there's people with a growth mindset, and they realize, 'I'm not the smartest person and I'm certainly not as smart as I could be, so even if I am the smartest person that ever lived, I could get a little bit smarter.' So when they're confronted with contradictory information, they learn and they soak it up like a sponge.

Everyone's on a spectrum, right? As much as I believe in it and work my a** off to have a growth mindset, I still have 10% where I catch myself. I'm like, 'Come on, dude. You know better than that.' So, for people that fall in under the 50% spectrum of the growth mindset, they have to catch themselves 98% of the time."

DO THIS TODAY: In what situations do you not have a growth mindset? Can you make that situation happen today? What will you say to yourself to get back into growth mindset mode? #254Action

Day 166:
Leo Gura

"My philosophy is that life is too short for dealing with difficult and talkative people. Life is already pretty challenging, you're already working really hard on your life, on your own self, why are you bringing yourself down with these talkative people?

My strategy ultimately is to get these people out of my life. I want people in my life who are supporting me, encouraging me, bringing in positivity. They're building something with me rather than going against me.

I really want to get to the root cause of it because I see people getting stuck in a social matrix. They're so worried about relying on various social relationships that they're not willing to get rid of these toxic people in their lives.

It creates this spiral of negativity that goes down and down brings you with it, and there's no need to live a life like that. You can't really self-actualize or create a powerful and happy fulfilling life if you're surrounding yourself with these types of folks.

One of the wisest things that Jim Rohn said was that you are the average of the top five associates that you hang out with.

This means that if you make a list of all the people in your life, and you write a number down for how many hours per week you're spending with each one of those people, and you rank everybody according to the number of hours you spend with them, the top five people that you spend the most time with are the people that have the most influence on you. It's a very simple theory.

Basically, whoever you hang out with is who you're going to absorb into yourself, and you become the average of all that. Then who do you want to surround yourself with? Positive, empowering people or negative, disempowering people?

If you do this exercise and you actually tally up the numbers, you might be shocked to discover that some of those people that you hang out with and spend five or 10 or even 20 hours a week with, that those are super negative, super pessimistic, super miserable, and depressive, anger-prone types of people.

Maybe that's why you're not getting the success you want in your life, because you're around these types of people all the time."

DO THIS TODAY: Try the exercise that Leo outlines in today's quote. Write down the top five people you spend time with and then evaluate if they have a positive or negative influence on you. #254Action

Day 167:

Robin Sharma

"Writing in a journal allows you to record your daily progress. There's a lot of scientific research on the small win theory. And what it says is this: If every single day, you record small daily acts of progress, you actually dump dopamine, a neurotransmitter, into your brain. And that is a great source of motivation. You'll feel happy and you'll feel strong and you'll feel inspired. It'll keep you motivated. It'll make you feel like you're making progress. It'll keep you inspired, versus always feeling like you're never achieving enough."

DO THIS TODAY: Every night before you go to bed, write down at least one win from the day, small or big. Every night. One win. #254Action

Day 168:
Brian Tracy

"Now once you've decided on the discipline you're going to develop, the key is for you to launch strongly. Resolve to never allow an exception until it becomes permanent. If you fall off the wagon, immediately restate your affirmation as a command to yourself and begin trying it again. This is the only way you could develop the habit of discipline in that particular area. The best part of this process of developing disciplines is the direct relationship between self-discipline and persistence. The more you persist in any endeavor, the greater self-discipline and self-confidence you'll develop. It's been well-said that persistence is self-discipline in action. The more consistently you practice your chosen disciplines, the more you will like and respect yourself. You will feel more confident and optimistic. You'll become more effective in every area of your life."

DO THIS TODAY: What's the discipline that you want to develop? Resolve today to never allow an exception until that discipline becomes permanent. #254Action

Day 169:

Dr. Ivan Joseph

"We all have this negative self-talk that plays in our heads. Guess what? There are enough people telling us we can't do it, that we are not good enough. Why do we want to tell ourselves that? We know for a fact that thoughts influence actions. Why do we want to say that negative self-talk to ourselves? We need to have our own self-affirmations. What was Muhammad Ali's self-affirmation? I am the greatest. Who else is going to tell you? There need to be quiet moments that we need to reaffirm, 'I am the captain of my ship and the master of my fate.' That is my affirmation. If I don't say it, if I don't believe it, no one else will. How do you build self-confidence? Get away from the people that will tear you down. There is enough of that.

The difference between hubris and ego, and false pride, is reminding yourself in quiet silent moments. I put it down in a list, it's right beside my mirror, about all the things that make me who I am, because I make enough mistakes and the newspapers will recognize it and people around me will recognize it and they will tear me down. Pretty soon I'll begin to believe it. There was a time when my confidence was pretty low. I wrote a letter to myself that was my own brag sheet about the things I was proud of, because there are moments in our career, in our life, in our job-hunting, in our relationships, when we are not feeling good about who and what and where we are. I had to bring out that letter and read it time and time again, for a period of about two weeks to weather me through that storm. Another example is, if you watch closely, you will see that some athletes have a bandage or a little brand around them. So put it on there and let's go."

DO THIS TODAY: Find a quiet moment and write out a list of why you're great. Write down at least 10 things. Then stick it to your bathroom mirror so you can see it every day. #254Action

Day 170:

Leo Gura

"Study success. Successful people study success. Success is not what we naively think of as something that happens naturally to some people and doesn't happen to other people. Success is a very deliberate, conscious endeavor that you undertake. Success is built over months and years and it's done consciously. The more you understand the principles of success, the concepts of success, the more you study people who have been successful, the more you see what it really takes. That process of success, the principles, are not always what they seem.

This is something that I've really committed my life to studying. I really love it. It's exciting for me. I really encourage you to get involved with it. That means attending some seminars, reading some books, watching videos, learning about it, maybe joining a group of friends that are successful, joining a mastermind group."

DO THIS TODAY: Try one of Leo's suggestions for studying success by reading or watching more material by one of your favorite thought leaders in this book. #254Action

Day 171:
Mel Robbins

"You know, I talk a lot about being honest with yourself about what you want. And if you're somebody that's watching this and you have no clue what you want, I'm going to say that's total bulls***.

I think you've probably decided that either you can't have it because you don't think you're smart enough or good enough or worthy enough, or maybe you think you're too old, or you've told yourself that you can't make a living doing it. Both are complete and utter lies that you're telling yourself.

What you need to do is ask yourself this: If you took money off the table, if you didn't give a s*** what anybody else thought, what's the thing you would love to be doing with your life?

Seriously? Do you dream of being a professional photographer? Do you want to open your own restaurant? Have you always thought about traveling the world and entertaining kids with your juggling skills?

I don't know, it's your life. You get to choose what you want to do. Be honest with yourself. What is it that you would want to do with your life if you didn't have to pay the bills doing it?

Another thing you can ask yourself: Who do you find yourself sort of envious of? You look at their life and you just think, 'Gosh, how awesome that they get to do that?'

Well once you have that answer for yourself, you've gotten really honest, you've pushed the bulls*** aside and you've really asked it for yourself and answered the question honestly, all you have to do is explore it.

That's it. Just find one thing that you can do to enrich and expand your knowledge about it, find one course online. Google the topic. Stalk people that are pursuing this line of work. That's how you start to do it. One step at a time.

DO THIS TODAY: Follow Mel's advice: "Start with answering the question what do you really want? With a massive dose of honesty. And find one thing that you can do, just one. Push yourself, and start to explore. If you were to wake up and do that every single day, spend 10 minutes a day, you would be startled, astonished by what your life looks like in a matter of a year." #254Action

Day 172:
Lord Alan Sugar

"I am very disciplined. A creature of habit in business and in life. I've worked on the principle of clearing my desk every minute or every day. Answering emails immediately, answering people's questions immediately. That's been my success in running my company, that I'm like a springboard for employees to tell me what their issue is, and then to give them a quick resolution, so they can get on and deal with it. That's my discipline, and I would heartily recommend to become disciplined. You should discipline yourself, because it's not a bad way of life."

DO THIS TODAY: Go to a cluttered area of your home or office and spend just ten minutes throwing things away and cleaning up. See how it makes you feel. #254Action

Day 173:
Robert F. Smith

"In my high school computer science course, they introduced this thing called a transistor, which is the building block of computers, and was invented at this place called Bell Labs, which had a facility about 20 miles from my home.

After that lesson, I called them and asked if they had summer internships, and they said, 'We absolutely do, if you're between your junior and senior year in college.' I said, 'I'm a junior in high school. I'm taking advanced math classes and computer science, just like being in college.' They said, 'No, it isn't.' So, I called every day for two weeks straight. Then I called every Monday for five months, and every time, the receptionist just chuckled, and she took my name, and she took my number, and she said, "We'll get back to you if there's an opening." And to my surprise, the HR director called my house and said, 'An intern from MIT didn't show up. We have an extra slot. We're not promising you anything, but why don't you come in and interview?' Now, I knew I was the most qualified candidate for this job. I interviewed, and I got it.

The persistence to get that job led to me working at Bell Labs for the next four years, becoming a co-op student, and ultimately finishing with a degree in chemical engineering from Cornell. All from being persistent."

DO THIS TODAY: Pick one goal and decide to be annoyingly persistent on it. Follow up every week until you get a positive reply. Pick just one goal and for the next year, follow up each week for 52 weeks and see what happens. #254Action

Day 174:
Brendon Burchard

"As you become more competent in something you learn how to do it, you're more confident in doing it. Psychologists often call this the confidence competence loop. As you learn how to ride a bike, and you rode the bike more and more, you became more skilled at it. You developed more confidence in your ability to ride the bike.

Any area of your life you're going to go into for the first time, be okay with being uncertain. Be okay with being uncomfortable. Be okay with not knowing how it's going to turn out, because it's your first time. But stumble into it anyway. Because if you stumble into it, you develop the skill. You develop comfort with it. And then suddenly one day you wake up and say, 'I'm pretty confident doing this.' Nothing changed in who you are. What changed is your level of competency, knowledge, skill, and ability. That's what competence is. When we finally realize, 'Oh wow, I just need to learn a little bit more here, I'll be more confident. I just need to apply this a little bit more here. I'll be more confident.' As you develop the skills and abilities in your life in your unique areas, you become more confident."

DO THIS TODAY: What is it that you want to get more confident in? Do something today to learn more about it and then practice it so you build momentum and feel the confidence that comes with competence. #254Action

Day 175:

John Maxwell

"I've never met a successful person that didn't have a great amount of self-discipline within their life. Self-discipline, being able to perform, being able to keep your life on schedule, and being able to keep commitments, promises, and meet deadlines, is essential to success.

None of us can afford to have a life that is controlled by someone else, or a life that is basically controlled by our emotions. I learned many years ago that there are two kinds of people: There's the type of person who says, 'I'm going to wait until I feel like it before I do it.' And then there's the person who says, 'I've got to do it so that I feel like it.' One will never get anything done, because they're still waiting to feel the moment to move, and the other person says, 'No, I need to move, and then I will begin to feel the moment.'

Assign yourself discipline. It's essential in your life if we're going to get things done."

DO THIS TODAY: This coming weekend, follow John's challenge to assign yourself discipline: "As you go through your weekend, as sometimes it's an easier time of your week, ask yourself, 'Am I practicing self-discipline in my life? Am I doing the things that I should do, because I need to do them, or am I kind of waiting to feel the moment?' Do like our friends at Nike say: Just do it." #254Action

Day 176:
Brendon Burchard

"Part of sustaining and making it through difficult times is maintaining hope. That isn't some airy fairy concept, it is a psychological need to believe that we can not only endure, but we can succeed, and we can thrive, and we can have our way in the world so that we can accomplish our dreams, so that we can influence, so we can make our own difference. Too many people say you have hope, or you can lose hope. But hope isn't something actually you have, or that you lose.

Years ago, a metaphor came into my life that changed my life forever. It was something that lifted me to a whole other level of joy and vibrancy in life, and it was very simple: The power plant doesn't have energy, it transforms and generates energy. At the same level, we don't 'have hope,' we transform the energy around us, we generate hope. We don't have happiness, we generate happiness. Similarly, we don't have sadness or fatigue. We don't have feelings that so many people think are negative just land on them. We are in our own actions, our own thoughts, our own interpretations. The very thoughts that we are feeding our psyche, those very things are generating an emotion. Hope is something that is generated by us. Just like when your phone is dying, you plug it in to charge it up. When your hope is dying, it's time to generate it and charge it up again. Same thing with happiness and enthusiasm and feeling alive. Those are things that, when they're going down, you've got to get focused, you've got to plug back in to your passions, to your dreams, to tomorrow."

DO THIS TODAY: It's time to generate some hope! Close your eyes and for 10 minutes don't focus on the million reasons why you're not going to make it and, rather, think about the eight ways that you will make it. #254Action

Day 177:

Azim Premji

"To make changes in any organization, you have to have a measure of very high persistency. You've got to go on, and on, and on, and on. When you don't have that persistency, very often you fall out just when success is around the corner."

DO THIS TODAY: Go to your calendar and schedule a time every day to spend time working on the thing you want more confidence in. It could be as simple as dedicating 15 minutes daily to do these exercises. The persistency will pay off. #254Action

Day 177 High Five!

Tennis Hall of Famer Martina Navratilova holds the all-time record for men or women with 177 doubles titles. You're at day 177 and are reaching rare territory. You're willing to do what most aren't. But you're not there yet. Let's keep going. High Five!

Day 178:

Sundar Pichai

"If at some point in your life, you have to work with people and you feel a bit insecure, that's essential because that means that you are working with people who are better than you, and who are pushing you. If you actually feel very secure in what you do, that means that you are doing something comfortable and you're not pushing yourself. There are many, many times I felt working with people in a group, 'Am I doing enough, are these people seeing much better than me?' and I think that's an inherent part of learning."

DO THIS TODAY: Do something today that makes you feel insecure. It could be making a phone call, booking a ticket to a convention, making a video... anything. The goal is to push your comfort zone and help you grow. #254Action

Day 179:

Robin Sharma

"Something that happens to most people is they reach a difficult part of their life and they call it failure. Just labeling a setback as a failure triggers something in your mindset to release cortisol, the fear hormone, which blocks your best performance. You want to study the alchemy, which is where other people are seeing a failure or a setback or even a little problem, and you want to look for the gold. You want to train your brain so you have a dominant belief and it becomes automatic because you've practiced it so much. Where someone says there's a problem or a failure you literally see the alchemy to turn the lead into gold. Maybe you're going through a divorce, maybe you're going through an illness, going through difficulties or outright tragedies. But you want to practice seeing the setback or the dark time as fuel to leverage your growth. Study the alchemy no matter what you are going through in your life, whether it's a large difficulty or a small setback. You want to ask yourself, 'How can I use what I'm going through as fuel for my growth? What is the gorgeous opportunity hidden inside this so-called problem?' If you look at the mass of humanity, they really train their brains to focus on problems. They hit a wall, and because of their belief system, they don't know it, because most people are not that aware of their belief systems. They blame it on the world, they blame it on the supplier, they blame it on the teammate, they blame it on their husband or wife, they blame it on their childhood, versus understanding our daily performance reflects our deepest beliefs. So, if you are experiencing some kind of setback, whether it's large or tiny, you want to train your brain to see the treasure within the lead."

DO THIS TODAY: What is the biggest 'problem' that you're facing right now. Then apply Robin's question: 'How can I use what I'm going through as fuel for my growth? What is the gorgeous opportunity hidden inside this so-called problem?' #254Action

Day 180:
Brendon Burchard

"Set up some social rewards. It's hard to stay disciplined at something if you're never getting any payoff from it. If you get some small wins along the way, and you're never celebrating with other people, then your brain says, 'Ah, this isn't benefiting me.' You must have that connection with others and celebrate, to keep your will intact, to keep doing the thing you're supposed to be doing.

It's so important for you to do this. You know if you're a writer and you finished a chapter, call up a friend and say, 'Hey, you know what? I finished the chapter I was supposed to finish today. Let's go out for a drink.' If you've accomplished something at work you said you were going to do, get everybody together and say, 'Hey, you know what? Lunch is on me today. Let me take care of you guys for lunch.' If you've finally achieved something that you've been working towards for so long, you need to take some time to go out with friends and family and just talk about the process. Talk about how it felt to finally complete this thing.

If we're never celebrating, we're never going to develop real discipline. It's funny, because too many people think those are opposite things. But the masters of this life have proven that doing things in a disciplined way can also be doing things in a joyful way. If you think discipline has to be this hard, awful, terrible thing, maybe you're never going to have discipline, because you're constantly trying to fool yourself into doing things you don't want to do. It's time to find the things that you do want to do."

DO THIS TODAY: What have you accomplished in the past week that you are proud of? Find something. Then celebrate it with someone in your life today. Feel the joy and momentum that it brings. #254Action

Day 181:

Reid Hoffman

"Maintain flexible persistence. Entrepreneurs are given two pieces of advice with equal vigor. If you look at them, they're in contradiction.

One is to have a vision. You'll plow through the wall. Keep your vision. Don't allow yourself to be unfocused from that. Keep going. The other one is, listen to your customers. Listen to market feedback. Listen to your network. Be really adaptive. How do you put those two things together?

It's a very difficult thing to teach other than by doing. Other than by the activity of going out and being an entrepreneur and making those decisions. The reason the rule is 'maintain flexible persistence,' is because it's both 'keep a vision' and 'be flexible.'

For example, if you think about the ABZ planning framework, it's like: 'Look, I've got a plan, I want to try to get there, this is my main plan. If that's hitting problems, like I'm not growing fast enough or I'm stalling out, okay, here are some things I can try to keep trying to do that. And if that doesn't work, how do I shift to a different destination, a different location?' That's part of the plan Z."

DO THIS TODAY: Be stubborn on the why and flexible on the how. Write down what our stubborn why is and then be open to how you get there because it will change many times over the next few years. #254Action

Day 182:

Marcus Lemonis

"I have a terrible fear that I lay awake at night with, and that's the fear of failure and the embarrassment that comes with it. People like to have a lot of pride and say, 'I'm not embarrassed, I'm not,' but I think anybody that's an entrepreneur, deep down, really deep down in their soul, has a fear of failure. 'What will people say, what will people think?'

And it's a hard challenge, and so I try to ignore it as much as I can, but I find it kind of haunting me. So I push through because I really believe that I have an obligation to keep trying and trying and trying, and I've had plenty of failure in my life. What happened was, when I turned 35, I became much more comfortable with admitting my vulnerability, acknowledging my mistakes, saying when I was wrong, showing my cards, and saying, 'Oh, that was stupid.' Crumbs could be one of those situations where I tried to outsmart something. Now, I don't think it's going to fail, but I have to be realistic. It could. Anything I do, could fail."

DO THIS TODAY: Share something with someone that you're embarrassed about. For me, I don't like being out of control of my body. So I've never been drunk, hate roller coasters, and don't fully participate at concerts. Now it's your turn. Find one of your vulnerabilities and share it with someone today. #254Action

Day 183:

Evan Carmichael

"When I was 20 years old I missed my shot at something because I was scared, and I vowed never to do it again. I was sitting with my map outside the Notre Dame Cathedral in Paris and a girl comes up and asks me for directions, but she was a French girl, and it didn't twig until later, why would a French girl be asking me for directions in English? Didn't really make sense, right? And then I thought, 'I should ask her out.' Just see what's she's doing tonight. I should ask her out for coffee or dinner or something. See what's she's up to. But I was afraid to do it and I let her walk away because really, I was afraid of rejection, and as she's walking away, the Notre Dame is on a river and I'm on one side of the river and she crosses over to the other side of the river, and I was so upset at myself. I was so upset that I didn't take my shot. I was so upset that I didn't at least try. I ended up taking a picture, but as I took it she actually walked behind one of the market stalls and I didn't actually get her picture.

So, I have this beautiful picture of this French riverside, and when I got home I was still upset about it. So I blew the picture up and I put it on my wall. It just looks like a nice, beautiful, French scene, but I didn't tell anybody what it really represented to me, why it was really so important, and I looked at that picture every day because the next time that I had to take my shot I wanted to go out and do it, I didn't want to be afraid. I wanted to conquer my fear and say, 'Yes!' And this served me really well a year or so later when I had to make a really tough decision: Do I take this job that I always wanted? I had these high-paying job opportunities with the companies that I really wanted, or continue with my startup that was failing, that was making $300 a month. The logical, practical, safe, easy thing to do would have been to take the salaried job. It's what I thought I always wanted. It's what my friends wanted. It's what you're supposed to do coming out of university. I didn't want to live with the regret of not knowing what happened with my business.

Looking at that picture daily reminded me to take my shot the next time it comes around, and I gave myself a year to say, 'I'm going to push off those jobs. I'm going to give this a shot. I can deal with the failure. I can deal with the rejection. I can deal with it not working out, even though that's a really short-term intense pain. What I can't deal with is the regret of not knowing because that's not some short-term minimal pain. That's forever.' If I chose not to focus on my business and I took that job I would forever look back on that moment and think, 'What if? What if I just tried a little bit harder? What if I gave it a little bit more? Yeah, but it wasn't working. I wasn't getting results, but what if I gave it a little bit more?' I did not want to live with that regret.

And I'm sure you've had moments in your life too, when you didn't take the shot, when you had an opportunity right in front of you and you didn't go for it. That picture on the wall helped me take my shot, and I hope sincerely that the next time you get your chance at something, that you don't shrink down. That you don't say no out of fear. That you don't say no because you find some practical reason why you can't do it. I hope that you take your shot, and if you've had those moments that you regret, where you wanted to take your shot and you didn't, give yourself a visual reminder like I did in my room to tell you, 'This is not happening again!'

Next time, I'm going to take my shot. I hope you take yours."

DO THIS TODAY: What was a shot that you missed taking? That you didn't do out of fear? Print off a visual reminder and stick it on the wall for the next week and see if it makes you more bold the next time an opportunity comes up and you're afraid. #254Action

Day 184:

Charlie Houpert

"If you want to convey honest confidence that inspires people, make sure you can back it up. As much confidence as Muhammad Ali had, and as much as he showed he was just as good in the ring, that wasn't everything that Ali had. He was also a dominant force in every interaction.

This kind of interaction might look insignificant, but it happens all the time and it is very important. It is a clash of frames. The winner of any frame collision is going to be the person who believes their frame more. These short little frame collisions happen all the time throughout your day in tons of different ways. And what's remarkable is that, from what I can tell, Mohammad Ali always stayed firmly rooted in his own frame. When we see that kind of conviction we can't help but be drawn to it.

Pay attention in your own life. In subtle little ways, who do you make adjustments for? And who do you stick to your guns with? That's a pretty clear indication of who the leader is in any sort of relationship. Now, there is no problem with taking a follower role sometimes. But in certain situations, like sales pitches, interviews, and even dates, you are usually going to benefit from being the leader. So those frame games become very important. Ali was so confident, had such a strong frame, that he seemingly had no fear of being honest. That might not seem like a big deal, but most people are extremely afraid of what others would think of them if they were totally real."

DO THIS TODAY: Think about who you make adjustments for in conversations. What do they do that allows their frame to win? What can you learn from them to bring into your other conversations? #254Action

Day 184 High Five!

In nuclear physics, 184 is believed to be a "magic number." You're magic too. I just wanted to tell you that. High Five!

Day 185:

Tony Robbins

"When it comes to planning your life I want to get you to learn to ask three questions now. The first one is not what am I going to do. It's what do I want? What's my outcome, what's my result? The word RPM, the first one is to get you focused on the target. The target is not the activity, the activity can change. It's the result I'm after. If you know exactly what it is you really want, what you desire, what you're really after. Clarity is power, the more clear you are in specifically what you want, the faster your brain can get you there. The way you language your goal, the way you think about it, you're receiving it. Because your brain is like a servile mechanism, if it knows the outcome, if it knows the result.

So RPM starts with R, I've got to know the result. This is a results planning system, the rapid planning method, but you can think of it as a results planning system. I need to know the result I'm after before I ever ask myself what to do. That takes more time, but its worth it. Something happens when you break an old pattern and you do it fresh. Your brain over the years has learned ways to move more rapidly. What is it that I really truly want from this? Just write those outcomes out. Not your action items. The outcomes. If you do that and nothing else, you will be ahead of the game. And if you just keep looking at those outcomes every day, how am I doing on that outcome? Your brain will come up with ways to get to that outcome. I promise you, focus on the outcomes, not on activities. Action for most people, activities, most people mistake movement for achievement. They mistake action items and to-do's for achievement. We are after the achievement.

Why is more important than how. Why are we doing this? What's the purpose? Purpose is more powerful than object. What's going to make you keep going? Purpose. Why is the most important thing to know because that's where all the emotional juice and fuel is to get you to go through when the challenges show up. Every person you see, who is on fire and is successful knows the why.

RPM. R is the result, the outcome, what you're after. P is the purpose. It's the why. 80% of success is why, 20% is how. Get a big enough why, people will figure out how to do it. I love it when I don't do my to-do's and I got the outcome, that's the coolest thing in the world. You might have done one or two of them, but it's then learning selectively which ones are going to create it. But the only way I knew how to do that is to brainstorm out the M, the massive action plan.

People do things for different reasons. People donate money for different reasons. But if you are going to work with a bunch of people you better make sure the why touches on all of their needs. If you know the result, and you know the purpose, now you need the M, which is the massive action plan. We also call the massive action plan the Map. It's your massive action plan, your Map. When you are crystal clear on what you want and you know why you want it, you can make a big Map, you can brainstorm a million ways to do it. Not all of your how's are going to work, that's why you make a whole Map and then go back and gradually asterisk the ones that are the most important and go hit those.

If you learn to put this on paper it'll be more powerful because your brain is erasing and you can see it. If you make it into a system that you personally use, your productivity will explode. If you teach your whole company to do this, your company will go to levels you can't even imagine, because everyone will maximize their productivity."

DO THIS TODAY: Do Tony's MAP exercise. Write out a list of 25 things you can do today to make progress on your goals. Then go back and asterisk the most important five. Today make sure you do something about those five. Let's go! #254Action

Day 186:
Evan Carmichael

"I like having a schedule. I like having a routine. I like having a calendar. I like having a list of habits. I like having a schedule for what I'm going to be doing every day, and I live and die by my calendar. I think it's really important. I think it keeps me on track. It keeps me focused. It keeps me somewhat regimented and I like that. I like that self-discipline that it imposes on me."

DO THIS TODAY: Create your routine. Create your calendar. Make sure your actions map to your ambitions. Put your ideal life in your calendar. Include your personal habits in there too. Then look at your calendar. If you did those things each week, would you be happy? Would you make progress on your goals? If no, adjust it again. Your actions must map your ambitions. #254Action

Day 187:
Chuck Norris

"Yeah I took acting classes. Even in my acting classes I couldn't get a part. I mean that's the truth! It was a struggle! How did I break through? I don't know, it's just determination, and not giving up, and persistence."

DO THIS TODAY: Think about one of your heroes and go find their startup story. Chances are they started with less than what you already have right now. Use their persistence, determination, and strategies to motivate you to action. If they could do it, so can you! #254Action

Day 188:

Steve Harvey

"A seed has to be planted. A seed has to have dirt put on top of it. If you take a seed and throw it on the concrete and walk off, the sun just burns it up. But guess what? Logically, in my mind, it doesn't make sense that to grow something where you should dig a hole, put it down in there, and cover it with dirt. See, dirt is necessary for growth and development. Dirt builds character. Dirt gives you the push-through factor. Dirt makes you come with it when you don't feel like coming with it no more. And you get dirt in a lot of different ways. Dirt isn't always what you want. It's somebody's talking about you on the job. It's somebody accusing you of something that you didn't do. It's somebody saying, 'You're not going to make it.' It's somebody sharing information about you that isn't true. That dirt builds character in you. It teaches you to withstand it, then it gives you something to push through, so when you put the seed down and you put the dirt on it, if you understand stress, stress really isn't just dirt. See, they don't call it dirt when they plant it. They call it soil because see soil has nutrients in it. Those experiences are actually putting nutrients in you. They're building character. You have character now. If they put a camera under the ground, you'd see the seed sprout open and start coming through the dirt because the dirt is necessary, so you can prove yourself. You know, everything you see above ground that blossoms and grows and that's beautiful, it was underground one time. They had to prove themselves. If you want to be successful, well then you've got to prove yourself. Push through the dirt. Come up through here. You got to come out, then you sprout, and then you become a tree. Next thing you know, you got fruit."

DO THIS TODAY: Make a list of five examples of how your seed is growing underground even though you haven't come through the dirt yet. What five things have you done that you're proud of and has built your character? #254Action

Day 189:
Amy Cuddy

"I want to start by offering you a free no-tech life hack, and all it requires is this: Change your posture for two minutes.

We make sweeping judgments and inferences from body language. And those judgments can predict really meaningful life outcomes like who we hire or promote, who we ask out on a date. So when we think of nonverbals, we think of how we judge others, how they judge us and what the outcomes are. We tend to forget, though, the other audience that's influenced by our nonverbals, and that's ourselves. We are also influenced by our nonverbals, our thoughts and our feelings and our physiology.

Do our nonverbals govern how we think and feel about ourselves? There's some evidence that they do. So, for example, we smile when we feel happy, but also, when we're forced to smile, it makes us feel happy. So it goes both ways. When it comes to power, it also goes both ways. So when you feel powerful, you're more likely to do this, but it's also possible that when you pretend to be powerful, you are more likely to actually feel powerful.

Powerful people tend to be, not surprisingly, more assertive and more confident, more optimistic. They actually feel they're going to win even at games of chance. They also tend to be able to think more abstractly. They take more risks. Power is also about how you react to stress. You want the person who's powerful and assertive and dominant, but not very stress reactive, the person who's laid back.

So when I tell people about this, that our bodies change our minds and our minds can change our behavior, and our behavior can change our outcomes, they say to me, 'It feels fake.' And so I want to say to you, don't fake it till you make it. Fake it till you become it. Do it enough until you actually become it and internalize. Tiny tweaks can lead to big changes.

So, this is two minutes. Two minutes, two minutes, two minutes. Before you go into the next stressful evaluative situation, for two minutes, try doing this, in the elevator, in a bathroom stall, at your desk behind closed doors. That's what you want to do. Configure your brain to cope the best in that situation. Don't leave that situation feeling like, oh, I didn't show them who I am. Leave that situation feeling like, I really feel like I got to say who I am and show who I am."

DO THIS TODAY: Do Amy's 'power posing' exercise. Watch her TED talk if you're interested in learning the science behind it! #254Action

Day 190:
CT Fletcher

"Unchain your mind. Unchain your mind from the imprisonment of fear. Unchain your mind. It's been caged with doubt. Unchain your mind. Lose yourself, let yourself free from the binds of average, from the binds of normal. Loose yourself from intimidation. Let yourself free, let your mind go. Shift your focus. Your focus, your intensity, your drive, your everything, should be put into the amount of effort that you are going to put into that attempt. You cannot fail. You cannot fail if you give 100% of your effort, mothers. You cannot fail. It is impossible. I don't remember the lady's name, but I remember her act. She came in absolutely last in the marathon. Everybody had crossed the finish line. She was the last person in the stadium, the lights were getting dark, and she fell down 25 yards before the finish line. But that lady effing crawled, she crawled. People tried to rush out and help her. The medics came out and tried to help her. She shooed them away. She shooed them away and she dragged her effing self across that finish line. That is the kind of attitude I want you to have. That's what you focus on. You focus on giving that mother everything you've got within you. Every drop of energy, every drop of strength, every drop of intensity. F what ifs. You always have power over the amount of effort that you put into whatever the F you are doing. Because the only mission I have, the only goals that I have, the only determination that I will make is that I'm going to give this mother every goddamn thing within me. Break the goddamn chains, break your chains, let yourself be free. Go out there and effing lay waste. Destroy some s***. Unchain your mind."

DO THIS TODAY: Write down five of your what ifs. Five of the things you're worried will happen if you take action. Then, next to each one, write down how you'll solve them if they come up. Most won't even happen, but if they do, you'll be ready. Now you're ready to act! #254Action

247

Day 191:
Michael Jordan

"If I had to trace my evolution, the Michael Jordan evolution, it always has to start back in college. Hitting the shot against Georgetown in 1982, and I really didn't know exactly what I was doing. It awakened a person inside of me to excel, to compete to excel, to be one of the best or be the best. That drove me, and with that shot, it ignited a fire inside of me that nothing was going to stop me."

DO THIS TODAY: What awakens the person inside of you that makes you want to compete to excel? Is it watching a video? Reading a book? Listening to a podcast? Schedule time for that thing in the first 10 minutes of your day. If you start your day feeling bold and unstoppable every day for the next year, your life will look unrecognizable from where you are right now. #254Action

Day 192:
Taraji P. Henson

"I was very nervous when I received the script for Cookie. She wasn't the most likable character, and I've played some pretty edgy characters, but this one was particularly a challenge, because it was prime time network television, and I wasn't sure how people would receive her. I mean, she beat her son with a broom, even though he deserved it. She called one son a faggot. It was scary, but, I'm the type of artist who believes that if the role doesn't scare me, I don't want it, because it's not going to change me as a person.

So, I took a risk, and that's what you do as an artist. You jump in feet-first and you see where it goes, and I knew that we had something special. I don't just jump feet-first for any project. I knew this was something special. I knew that what Fox was trying to do, what Lee Daniels and Danny Strong were trying to do, and what I was trying to do was shake up television. It's too safe. Life is not safe and I think we did that with this show. I'm so proud to be a part of this project, and I'm so proud that Fox believed in us and took a chance, because that's what art is about. Taking chances, taking risks."

DO THIS TODAY: Think about what's in your calendar this week. Does anything scare you? If not, how can you inject something in that will? If you don't have anything that scares you, you're not growing. #254Action

Day 192 High Five!

Polish-made Spirytus vodka is 192-proof. It's the strongest bottle of liquor sold in the world. With the strength you're building here you'll soon be the stronger person in your community and able to lift everyone around you up. High Five!

Day 193:

Simon Sinek

"Here's the problem with my stuff, you've got to do it. And I'm not anybody's mom or dad. I'm not going to do it for you, and I have a very laissez-faire approach to it. I once had a client that said, 'What guarantee do I have that your stuff will work?' To which my answer was, 'None!'

I'm giving you a tool. It's like a hammer. You can use it broadly or narrowly. You can build a table, or you can build a house. It's the same tool. You can use it for marketing, or you can use it to completely revitalize your entire culture. And even though I'm going to sell you the most beautiful hammer, I'm not going to guarantee the structural integrity of the house.

It's your business. You want to ignore all my stuff? Ignore it! I don't care! And if your business collapses, you know what happens to me? Nothing!

I don't mean to be cold about it. Of course I want the people I work with to do well, but it's not mine. It's theirs, and I take no emotional responsibility for the decisions they make. There are many people that I've had the pleasure of working with.

Some who worked for dysfunctional organizations that went on the hard journey of completely changing the way they lead and completely revitalizing their culture. And they had great success. It's not because of me. It's because of them.

Especially in the consulting world or the design world, everybody's so paternalistic about it. And designers are famous for this. They get so personally offended when the client chooses the wrong thing: 'Ooh, such idiots, don't they know we're trying to help them?' Or, 'Who cares? Like, it's their fricking business!'

But instead of arguing with somebody for them to make the right choice because we genuinely want to help them, what I have found is to push the accountability onto them.

When we argue, we're taking accountability. If we say, 'Look, we've been doing this a bunch of years. We know more about design than you do. I'm telling you, for every reason that I can outline for you, why this will help you more, but if you don't want to do it? That's fine. It's your business. Do what you want.'

The minute you switch the accountability and put it all on them, amazingly, they're much more open to your opinion."

DO THIS TODAY: Think about who you've been trying to help that isn't taking your advice. Close your eyes and spend five minutes to release them from your expectations. It's their life and their choice. #254Action

Day 194:

Aaron Marino

"Compliment others. How does it feel getting a compliment? It feels incredible. It also feels incredible giving them. Here's the interesting thing about compliments. When somebody gives you a compliment, you automatically like them more, right?

The follow-along is the person getting the compliment feels incredible, you feel great for making them feel incredible, and they actually like you more.

The other upside to giving compliments is that it helps you develop your people skills, getting to confidence and increased social prowess."

DO THIS TODAY: Find three people today and give them a genuine complement. Feel how great you both feel afterwards. #254Action

Day 195:
Pierre Omidyar

"When you look at the accomplishments of accomplished people, and when you look at something that looks hard, that was probably easy. And conversely, when you look at something that looks easy, that was probably hard. So you're never going to know which is which until you actually go and do it.

So just go and do it, try and learn from it. You'll fail at some things, but that's a learning experience that you need so that you can take that on to the next experience. And don't let people who you may respect, and who you believe know what they're talking about, don't let them tell you it can't be done, because often they will tell you it can't be done, and it's just because they don't have the courage to try it."

DO THIS TODAY: Write down the goal that people around you (or you) are saying can't be done. Then close your eyes for two minutes and summon the most courageous version of yourself. Open your eyes and write down underneath how you're going to get that goal done. #254Action

Day 196:

Robert Rodriguez

"You can't just wait for inspiration to act. That's the biggest mistake people make. Don't wait to be inspired to do the action. You have to do the action first, and then you'll be inspired.

So, what I would do is, I would sit there and I would draw the comic and I would come up with it. Some days I would come home from school, sit down, and go, 'I'm just going to wait for the inspiration to hit me. I'm going to wait for the idea to come fully formed. And when I got a joke then I'll go draw it.' And I would sit there for maybe three or four hours and go alright, 'Screw it, I've got to get up and I've got to do the process. I've got to sit there and just start drawing. I don't even know why or how I'm going to get there.' And then two things would come together, and it'd be, 'Oh there's an idea. Oh there's the first panel, there's the second panel.' And then it would come together always. It would not take very long.

I would fight that process so much, because what was I doing? I was waiting for inspiration before I acted. It's always the other way around. Act first, then the inspiration will come. Draw first, then the inspiration will come. Just start shooting, then the inspiration will come. Just start moving, then the inspiration will come. Don't wait. So many people wait or tell you they're going to write this novel or they're going to make this film. They never do it because they're waiting for all this stuff to come to them. It comes through doing it."

DO THIS TODAY: Pick something on your goal list and just attack it today. Don't worry about being inspired. Just start. There is no perfect first step. Just take any step. Build momentum. And from that momentum something great will happen for you. #254Action

Day 197:
Brendon Burchard

"Humanity develops in its psyche. We develop a real extensive competence or confidence coming from a sense of integrity for ourselves.

Integrity is, 'I know who I am and I am being that consistently. I know what I want and I am chasing that consistently.' Being aligned with who you are, your values, your beliefs and your dreams, having integrity. That gives us confidence in self. That gives us a sense of confidence.

How've you been doing in that department? Have you been really demonstrating who you are to the world? Have you allowed yourself to do that? Because if you do that over a period of time, the self and I would argue the soul senses a coherence. There's a cohesive sense of identity that comes from being consistent to the best of who we are. Confidence comes from that, and that too is a will, it is a decision, it is a desire to want to be a person of integrity and confidence and that's where it stems from."

DO THIS TODAY: What is your One-Word-single-most-important-core-value? Write it down. Look at day today and tomorrow and think about how you can incorporate your One Word into all your activities? #254Action

Day 198:

Gary Vaynerchuck

"We've all failed. It's easy for me to be happy. I have my s*** in the right order. The health and wellbeing of my family, and there's nothing even remotely close to that. People have gone through much worse. This is why I'm trying to recall our grandparents and our great-grandparents. People were persecuted and killed. We do not have real headaches.

I don't know why I have this highly emotional and then completely unemotional part of me, but I mix them together to create the balance, and that's what works for me. So of course, there's nothing that I couldn't get up from. Like every other human ever. We are strong as s***. We're really effing strong. We're just being sold that we're not, because there's a lot of money in telling us that we're not pretty enough, thin enough, smart enough, good enough. F that. I want to tell you, you're the effing best. Go do s***."

DO THIS TODAY: Write down five reasons why you're strong. Read the list back and feel strong. #254Action

Day 199:
Nas

"Push yourself all the way. Don't obsess over what anybody else is doing. If you're given the opportunity and you're lucky enough to have freedom to do what you want to do in your career, why trap yourself? Why do something that's not you?"

DO THIS TODAY: Think about someone you're jealous or envious of. Think about how you can use them as an inspirational kick forward instead of a demotivating kick down for yourself. #254Action

Day 200:
Andy Frisella

"You know what? I'm going to tell you something right now. You should effing quit. And you know what you should quit? You should quit effing quitting, all right?

I want you to think about something, and I want you to think about it in terms of your life. If you wanted to run a marathon, but every time you got frustrated, every time you got tired, every time you got winded, every time you got sore, you turned around and went back to the starting line and started over, because of all these things that are painful, would you ever complete the goal of running a marathon? Of course not.

Life is the same. Success is the same. Nothing worthwhile is going to be given to you. It's going to be earned, and it's going to be earned through your pain, through your misery, through your suffering. None of it's going to be effing easy, guys. And the factor that separates almost every single person in life that's been successful, is people that succeed quit effing quitting when things get hard.

Quitting is a habit, okay? Quitting is a mentality, it's a core value of people. They get a little bit down the road, and either they don't finish, or they say, 'Man, this is hard, I'm going to try something else.' You know, 'This isn't for me, because it's effing hard.' It's all effing hard! That's what you don't understand. Any path you take to get where you want to be, if that place is worthwhile to go, it's going to be effing hard.

So quit judging your quitting, or your wanting to do something else based upon how hard something is. Because every single path that you could possibly take to get somewhere where you want to be is going to be hard. That's just a fact of reality of this earth, okay?

But that's what you have to understand. Struggle, pain, misery, frustration. Those are signs that you are a) on the right path and b) making progress. You have to learn to identify these things as indications that you are on the right path, okay? Nobody that is where you want to be has gotten there without these struggles, without the bleeding, without the pain, without the depression, without the misery. Nobody.

So what makes you think that you're going to be able to be that person that gets there with none of those things? Guys, life is hard. Success is really effing hard. And if you want to be something big, you want to dream big, you want to be something great, you are going to have to learn to accept the struggle as part of the recipe.

Every single day you need to look yourself in the mirror and ask yourself, 'What am I willing to do to get what I want?' And if the answer is 'Whatever the F I have to,' you'll probably get there in time. But if it's anything less, you won't. And that's just a fact of life."

DO THIS TODAY: Summon the most confident version of yourself and go to the mirror. Ask yourself 'What am I willing to do to get what I want?' Respond with courage. #254Action

Day 201:

Evan Carmichael

"You have to love what you're doing. You have to love the process, because you can only force yourself to do things that you don't like for so long. If you hate the idea of working out or going to make those cold calls or creating content for YouTube, if you hate doing it, you can create a calendar and a schedule and a routine, you can put it on Google Calendar and you can say, 'I have to get this done every day,' and you'll do it for a certain amount of time, but at some point, you can only do something that you hate for so long before something breaks, before something gives and you have to change. Yes, the schedule and the tools can help you, but at the top, you have to actually love what you're doing and if you don't love it, then find another way to stand, find something that you do love, find something that makes you come alive, because it's way easier to stay disciplined about something when you love the process and not just the end result."

DO THIS TODAY: Look at your calendar and the tasks that you have to do. How can you inject more passion, joy, and creativity to them? #254Action

Day 202:

Mike Tyson

"When I come out of the dressing room I have supreme confidence, but I'm actually scared to death. I'm totally afraid. I'm afraid of everything. I'm afraid of losing, I'm afraid of being humiliated, but I am totally confident. The closer I get to the ring, the more confident I get. All during my training I've been afraid of this man. I thought this man might be capable of beating me. I've always stayed afraid of him, but the closer I get to the ring, the more confident I am.

Once I'm in the ring I'm a god, no one could beat me. I walk around the ring but I never take my eyes off my opponent. I keep my eyes on him, even if he's ready and pumped and he can't wait to get his hands on me. I keep my eyes on him, then once I see his chink in his armor, boom! One of his eyes may move, then I know I have him. Then when he comes to the center of the ring he still looks at me with his piercing look as if he's not afraid, but he already made that mistake when he looked down for that one-tenth of a second. I know I had him. He'll fight hard for the first two or three rounds but I know I already broke his spirit. During the fight, I'm supremely confident. I'm moving my head, he's throwing punches, I'm making him miss and I'm countering. I'm hitting him to the body, I'm punching him real hard and when I'm punching I know he's not able to take my punches. One, two, three punches. I'm throwing him punches in bunches.

He goes down, he's out. I'm victorious. Mike Tyson, greatest fighter that ever lived."

DO THIS TODAY: Create a ritual that you can do every morning that will transform you from afraid to confident. What needs to happen for you to make that transformation daily? #254Action

Day 203:
Neil Gaiman

"If you want to write stories, start writing stories. Really, it's as simple as that. Pick a style, pick a theme. You are not expected straight out of the bat to be a brave and original voice, producing fine and wonderful fiction. It's much more like the first pancake on the griddle which is going to be this weird, black, messy thing that you will give to your dog, or to a child, trying to convince them it's nice. You'll write. You'll finish things. You start the next thing. You write that, you finish it. Somewhere in there, you get reasonably good.

The point I always found that I would learn more about what I'd done was the moment I saw it in print. Or these days, probably the moment you'd see things up on the Web. But yeah, show them to people. The most important thing when you're just starting out is to write the next one. Assume that you have a million words inside you that are absolutely rubbish, and you need to get them out before you get to the good ones. And if you get there early, that's great. That's really my biggest advice. Read everything you can. Read outside your comfort zone. And write a lot."

DO THIS TODAY: Block off five hours in the next week to practice, practice, practice the thing you want to get better at. Feel the confidence that comes from taking action and improving. #254Action

Day 204:
Natalie Portman

"People told me that Black Swan was an artistic risk, a scary challenge to try to portray a professional ballet dancer. But it didn't feel like courage or daring drew me to it. I was so oblivious to my own limits that I did things I was woefully unprepared to do, and so the very inexperience that in college had made me feel insecure, and made me want to play by others' rules, now was making me actually take risks I didn't even realize were risks.

When Darren asked me if I could do ballet, I told him that I was basically a ballerina, which by the way, I wholeheartedly believed. When it quickly became clear in preparing for the film that I was maybe 15 years away from being a ballerina, it made me work a million times harder, and of course, the magic of cinema and body doubles helped the final effect. But the point is, if I would have known my own limitations, I never would have taken the risk. And the risk led to one of my greatest artistic and personal experiences, and I not only felt completely free, I also met my husband during filming."

DO THIS TODAY: Think of your greatest limitation. Now imagine that you were free from it. That you could do the thing you were terrified to do. Feel the power of it and now take one small action step towards making it happen. #254Action

Day 205:
Wayne Dyer

"Have a mind that is open to everything and attached to nothing. One of the central principles of my life is that no one knows enough to be a pessimist about anything. That each and every one of us, when we close our mind to what is possible for us or what is possible for humanity, closes off the genius that resides and lives in each and every one of us. Having an open mind doesn't necessarily mean finding fault with all of the things you've been taught by others, it means opening yourself up to the potentiality, that anything and everything is possible.

Having a mind that is open to everything and attached to nothing really means finding the ability within ourselves to get rid of a trait that I find so common in the contemporary world: Most people that I meet spend their lives looking for occasions to be offended. They actually are out there hoping that they can find some reason to be offended and there's no shortage of reasons. They are out there, everywhere. The way this person dressed, the thing this person said. They turn on the TV, they hear the news, they're offended. Someone used language they didn't like, someone doesn't share the same customs. In fact, all day long, if you keep track tomorrow, you will probably find 100 reasons that you could go around being offended.

But a mind that is open to everything and attached to nothing is a mind that says, 'I'm never looking for anything to be offended by.' And whatever anybody else out there has to say, my response to that is, 'That's an interesting point of view. I've never considered that before.'"

DO THIS TODAY: Think of someone who has wronged or offended you. Picture them in your mind. Now, consider what they did to you. Tell yourself, "That's an interesting point of view. I've never considered that before." How do you feel? #254Action

Day 206:
Evan Carmichael

"The more you practice, the better you're going to get. I practice my YouTube videos and I've gotten better at making YouTube videos. Go back to my channel, and you'll see the results. I practice at snowboarding, and I've gotten to be a better snowboarder. Anything you practice at, you're going to get better at. You practice a language, you're going to improve your language skills. You practice marketing, you're going to improve your marketing skills. Practice, practice, practice leads to results and knowing that you can do it leads to confidence you can do it again and take the next bigger step.

Think of it like a ladder. If you're at the bottom and you want to go to the top, that may seem like a huge challenge, but going two rungs up may not be so big. And when you get there, you can go four rungs up. And then you can go eight rungs up, on and on. And then you look down and suddenly you've covered a huge distance. So, practice definitely helps."

DO THIS TODAY: What can you do today, if only for five minutes, to practice the thing that you want to get more confident at? #254Action

Day 206 High Five!

Socio-economist Randal Bell studied successful people for decades and said that those who make their bed in the morning are up to 206.8% more likely to be millionaires because it puts your mind into a productive mindset. This book is your daily mindset boost. Don't stop now. We're almost there. High Five!

Day 207:
T. I.

"Nothing in life worth having comes free. Nobody's going to give anybody anything. Now, you get out of life what you're willing to put into it. Hard work, sacrifice, dedication, all of these things breed success.

I can tell you this because I was once one of the people who were assumed to be less likely to become successful. I'm from a very modest neighborhood. I didn't necessarily grow up with a silver spoon in my mouth. I didn't have all the things that I wanted. Sometimes not even all the things that I needed.

But it's important for you to know your environment does not define you unless you allow it to. The position that you're in right now does not dictate your future unless you allow it to. You can look at your life as it is right now and could say, 'I'm not where I want to be. This isn't where my life will end.'

You can do one of two things: You could use it as an excuse to do nothing, or you could use it as motivation to push yourself forward. The choice is yours.

I need you to understand and believe that anything in life is possible. Whatever it is you want to do is absolutely possible. I don't care how much trouble you've gotten into up unto now. I don't care how many things you may have done wrong. I don't care how much you may not have in your life to help you.

You can do it. If you believe in yourself enough to make it happen. If you put enough effort and energy and invest enough in your future, you can do anything in this world you want to do. Anything's possible. Don't never let nobody tell you what you can't do.

I started rapping when I was nine years old. And I'm from Atlanta. At the time when I was rapping, there weren't any other rappers in Atlanta. I heard every excuse why I couldn't be a rapper. I heard every excuse why I couldn't be famous. Everything from, 'You can't rap' to 'You're too skinny' and 'Nobody from the south makes it big and goes platinum.'

I heard all these things, a whole bunch of excuses, a whole bunch of reasons why I should not believe that I could make it. But my belief overcame that doubt because I believed in myself. And if I could do it, you can do it."

DO THIS TODAY: Make a list of all the "reasons" why you can't accomplish your goal. Write them down. Then put a huge X through it, tear the paper to pieces, and throw it in the recycling bin. Release them. Now write down why you will accomplish your goal. #254Action

Day 208:
Al Pacino

"My instincts, I always felt, were better earlier in my life than they are now. It seems as though sometimes I'm a little bit blinded by the attention, so I don't make correct assessments. I'm a little bit influenced by the fact that I'm not on the outside, looking in. I was fortunate enough to have certain things happen in my life. And persisting in a thing, you know? I think the saying goes, 'He who persists in his folly will one day be wise.' I haven't gotten wise yet but I keep persisting."

DO THIS TODAY: When you don't feel like persisting, what will you do? Create a plan for yourself so that even if you don't feel like doing something, you'll still do it and you'll move closer to reaching your goal. #254Action

Day 209:
Brendon Burchard

"Keep your perspective as being a champion of humanity. What do I mean by that? Oftentimes, when we're frustrated with other people, we've lost our connection with humanity in some way or another. We're in a big hurry and we've forgotten that people have stories and realities that we do not know about.

You don't know what is going on in somebody's day when they just pissed you off. They just did something and you think, 'Oh, well. They're like this.' Maybe you had a co-worker who was supposed to deliver something in the morning and they didn't deliver. Now you're fired up and you're frustrated about them. But sometimes you don't know the real challenge and frustrations people are dealing with at their home, in their regular life with their family. You don't know.

See, we make all these assumptions about people and we never know their real story. And soon as you lose your patience with people, you lose your connection with humanity. You lose that understanding that stuff happens in people's lives. As busy, as stress-filled as you are, other people have that, too. And if you don't believe that, then you've gotten to a place where you've allowed your intellect to grow your ego to such a level that you can't connect with humanity anymore. What happens for so many people is they do. Especially folks who are 'intellectuals,' people who feel like they're very evolved, enlightened, supremely conscious. What ends up happening for them is sometimes they have lost that real connection because they think they're so special versus other people.

Ultimately, here's the challenge with folks who do have an ego like that or who do feel so much more supremely special than other people: They become very caged in their lives. It's like watching an animal that is caged, that gets resigned, because it's been wild and free at some point and now it's resigned in the back of the cage, curled up, angry and frustrated, pointing at people. 'They don't understand me.' And the folks who often say that are the same people who rarely ever raise their hand and ask for help. They're the folks who easily get frustrated, annoyed, or resigned from other people. And when they need help, or when they want to progress their life, because they've drawn away from others, they believe other people can't understand them. So they don't ask for help. They don't collaborate. They don't socialize. They don't create the very influence, relationships, and networks that are necessary for them to grow to the next level in their life and in their business.

Think about that for a moment. Have you become so disconnected from other people that you're often frustrated with them, because you forgot you don't understand their story? You don't know what they're going through. Just like when you're saying, 'They don't know what I'm going through,' everybody else feels that way. Once you understand that the reality of humanity is just a bunch of human beings walking around with signs on top of their heads saying, 'Please understand me,' 'please be patient with me,' 'please help,' then you stop getting frustrated with people. And you realize we're all struggling. We're all doing the best that we can. We all have big dreams and goals and desires. Being connected to humanity is learning to be patient with people again."

DO THIS TODAY: Write down the names of three people you are going to be more patient with and try to better understand their story. #254Action

Day 210:
Mark Zuckerberg

"In a world that's changing so quickly, the biggest risk you can take is not taking any risk. And I really think that's true.

A lot of people think that whenever you get yourself into a position where you have to make some big shift in a new direction or do something. There are always people who are going to point to the downside risks of that decision. And locally, they may be right. For any given decision that you're going to make, there's upside and downside. But on aggregate, if you are stagnant and you don't make those changes, then I think you're guaranteed to fail and not catch up.

So, the biggest risk that you can take is to not take any risks."

DO THIS TODAY: What risk do you want to take but you're afraid to jump into? Now think about everything you will lose out on for the rest of your life if you stay where you are and don't summon the strength to take that risk. #254Action

Day 211:
Evan Carmichael

"How do you get that confidence? Some people may be born with it. For me, it was much more about changing my environment. I got some confidence from my parents. 'Believe' came from them. They always told me I could do whatever I wanted, and that gave me a sense of confidence. But if I look into my entrepreneurial career, a lot of it came from my habits and what I was reading, and now later, the videos. By surrounding myself with people that are confident, that are doing big things, and not necessarily in my actual life. I don't have a ton of super-successful, super-confident friends that I hang around with. It's much more from aspirational mentors.

I created the YouTube channel and The Top 10 Rules, in part, selfishly for myself, to be around greatness, to be around success on a regular basis. You can do that for yourself as well. If you want to develop confidence, I think a lot of it comes from your environment, from osmosis, just by being around confident people. Some of that wears off on you. It's why I started the #MentorMe series. Let's hang around people that have done a lot more than us, and some of their mindsets and their beliefs and the way that they think about things seeps into us to help us become the best version of ourselves, not to be the next Elon Musk or Steve Jobs or whoever, but a more confident, better version of ourselves.

There was a point where it really struck me. I was driving with my father in the car, and I just signed a deal with a CEO who runs a multi-billion dollar company with nearly 15,000 employees. We're both doing this Q&A. We're answering questions, I'm hosting the show. We get a question from an entrepreneur. He answers it, I answer it. And my dad asked me, 'How do you get the confidence to be on par with this big CEO, that you're his equal, That you're answering questions alongside him?' It wasn't in a 'you-suck' kind of tone. It was a general admiration, in a very supportive way. I thought about it and it's really from the videos. It's really from all this work, because I'm hanging around Elon Musk and Kanye West and Snoop Dogg and Martha Stewart, and all of these successful people. Whether they're athletes or musicians or entrepreneurs. I'm around that constantly, and so seeing people being confident and going off and doing great things makes me be more confident.

So by hanging around greatness more, you unleash a little bit more greatness inside of yourself as well, and the more you do that, and the more consistent you are with that, then the 'more' is going to come out. I agree that a poor man with confidence will be unstoppable. The question then becomes how do you get that confidence, and if you weren't born with it, I think that's okay. I think there's so much you can do by changing your habits, by changing your environment, by surrounding yourself with resources, information, videos, guides of confident successful people that will unleash that inner boldness in you, to go off and do amazing things."

DO THIS TODAY: You're already building your confidence exposure by reading this book every day. Now stay consistent. Don't miss a day and fall back into your old habits and patterns of thinking. #254Action

Day 212:

Tony Robbins

"Here's what I've created for my life and anyone I know who succeeded. I was a 17-year-old kid from Azusa, California with no real education other than self-education. With no background, with parents that did their best. With no money. But I did one thing. I loved people, and I had an enormous demand I made upon myself, and I sculpted my mind and my emotions to get me to do whatever it would take to achieve and to contribute. I did it by using my body and changing my focus. I did it by putting myself in a peak physiology and using what I called incantations.

Can you train yourself to believe something? Absolutely. Have you ever made the fatal mistake of going to Disneyland or Disney World, and while you're there, made the fatal mistake of going on a ride called 'It's A Small World After All?' What happens for about a week after you're out of that damn place? You're still singing this song in your head in 24 languages, right? Well, let me tell you something. How many of you have times when you want to go achieve things and this voice goes, 'Oh it's not going to happen,' or 'forget it?' A voice that sometimes interrupts that good pattern. You want to train a new one.

So, starting when I was 17 I started doing incantations. Not affirmations. Affirmations make you go, 'I'm happy, I'm happy, I'm happy, I'm happy, I'm happy.' What's the problem? You haven't changed your physiology. If you don't change your physiology, you won't get anything. So, in incantations, not only you speak it, you embody what you're saying with all the intensity you can and you do it with enough repetitions that it sticks in your head. Like 'It's A Small World,' now the conversation in your head is always the same and it gives you what you want. So, use your body and your voice. #254Action

I do an incantation using my whole body. I say, 'I now command my subconscious mind to direct me in helping as many people's possible lives today, to better their lives by giving me the strength, the emotion, the persuasion, the humor, the brevity, whatever it takes to show these people and get these people to change their lives now.' When two people meet, if there's rapport, the person that's the most certain will always influence the other person. And I was totally certain and they were trying to get revved up to certainty.

I did another to change my mindset. I used to keep doing things but I never got beyond it. I'd say, 'God's wealth is circulating in my life. It's what flows to me in avalanches of abundance. All my needs, desires, and goals are met instantaneously by infinite intelligence. For I'm one with God and God's everything.' And I would imagine the abundance in my life and I would feel so grateful. And a year after I started at 17, I went from making $38,000 a year to making a million dollars a year."

DO THIS TODAY: Write out an incantation that makes you feel confident. Speak it aloud using your whole body.

Day 212 High Five!

In Fahrenheit, 212 degrees is the boiling point of water at sea level. You're about to boil over into becoming a new person. Can you feel it? It's happening. You're stronger, wiser, more confident than when you started. You're never going back to where you were before. High Five!

Day 213:

Bishop T. D. Jakes

"Life demands that you pick up the pace. If you don't pick up the pace, you're going to be left behind. I'm amazed at the people that lack the flexibility to pick up the pace. They just get in a rut.

One of the most amazing things about the disaster in Malaysia is that when it happened, everybody had to pick up the pace. All the news media had to pick up the pace. They were booking night flights, and flying over here, and flying over there. Somebody had to work overtime. Won't be home for three days. Typing in the middle of the night. Research going on.

Because, when something happens, everybody's got to pick up the pace. Slap your neighbor and say, 'Pick up the pace!' Something's about to happen, pick up the pace. Something is about to happen, I came to tell the young people. 'Pick up the pace! Pick up the pace! Pick up the pace! Something is about to happen!'

The danger of low expectations: I would rather aim for the stars, and not hit them, then to not aim at all. I would rather go after it, and not get it, than not go after it at all. I'd rather try and fail, than not try at all.

I don't want to live with the idea, wonder what would have happened had I done more with my life. I'm going to go for it, come hell or high water, I'm going after my destiny.

Touch your neighbor, and say 'Run!' You've got to run after your destiny. You can't stroll after your destiny. You can't walk after your destiny. You've got to run!

You can't just wake up in the morning and say, 'Let me see what's going to happen today. Ah, I don't know what I'm going to do, I don't know what I'm going to wear, I don't know what I'm going to cook. I don't know where I'm going to go. I just woke up, oh, I should stay in the bed.'

Give the day to somebody who's going to run after their destiny. Give the day to someone who has a plan, who has a strategy. Because success is never an accident. And, if you don't want it, get out of my way! Because there are some people who want to do something with their life. Who will run."

DO THIS TODAY: Write down three things you're doing to do in the next 24 hours to pick up the pace and run after your destiny! #254Action

Day 214:
Travis Kalanick

"The champions mindset: First, when a lot of people hear the word 'champion,' they think of a famous sports star. In the US, you might think of Michael Jordan or LeBron James going and dunking on somebody. But we think of it differently. We think of it as when you get on the field, put everything you have into it. Put every ounce of energy you have on the field. Leave nothing on the field.

Second, when you get knocked down, because if you're an entrepreneur inevitably you will be, when you see hard times and you get knocked down, get back up. And if you keep putting everything you've got into it, and you keep getting back up when you get knocked down, it's almost impossible to fail."

DO THIS TODAY: Study one of your heroes and learn their story. The next time you get knocked down, look at their story. Know that you're not alone and if you keep getting back up, you'll achieve your goals too. #254Action

Day 215:
Oprah Winfrey

"Assertion is not negative. Being assertive is not being negative. There's a difference between the intention of being negative and the intention of being assertive. Part of this journey is learning to stand on your own two feet. When you're assertive, sometimes you get the very things that you're standing up for.

DO THIS TODAY: Think where you need to be more assertive in your life. Who do you need to have an honest conversation with to let them know how you feel and how can you frame it so it's assertive but not negative. Practice the conversation out loud. #254Action

Day 216:
Evan Carmichael

"Have a mastermind group. The idea here is you have people around you who are pushing you to be better, who believe in you, who can see the negative self-talk in you, who have your best interests at mind, who understand what your goals are, and try to gently or sometimes not so gently, push you in that direction.

I've run mastermind groups for entrepreneurs here in Toronto for the past 10 years or so. The reason why you're not doing the thing that you're supposed to do, to help get your business where it's supposed to be, is usually a limiting personal belief. And you are probably not recognizing that. Having people around you to call you on your own BS, when you're giving a practical, reasonable answer, but they know that it's just BS, that really helps.

It could be a formal structure where you have people meet every month, that's what we do, and there's between six and eight of us, depending on the size of the group. Or it could just be a friend of yours, or it could be people in your industry that you want to connect with on a regular basis. You want people around you to help push you to be that best version of yourself, and give you the confidence that you sometimes need to make the tough decisions when you don't have the confidence yourself."

DO THIS TODAY: Make a list of three people who would be a good potential fit for your own group. Reach out to them today to see if they're interested. #254Action

Day 217:

Brendon Burchard

"What is it you're really after, and are you after enough for yourself? Are you limiting yourself based on your current competencies? A lot of people do that. They narrow their vision or ambition for tomorrow based on what they can do today, or who they are today, without realizing they can develop their mastery, their skills, their competency, their knowledge, their experience, without realizing they can become a better person.

They can become their highest self, they can become the type of person who could accomplish those goals, who could have those things, so never limit your ambitions based on your current competencies. Never limit yourself today based on your current inadequacies because those can be irrelevant tomorrow. The main thing is to have an aim in life, to have your own goal, to have your own ambitions, not the ambitions somebody said you should have, or someone said you're supposed to be after. Because that's how we get on a corporate treadmill. Or we get on those things where we start trying to live a life that's not even our own because we're just going with everybody.

But ambition liberates that. Your individual ambition, who you want to become, what you want to do, what you want to contribute, and the highest forms of all ambition usually come down to your creative expression, your contribution, and your connection with others. That creative expression, what is it you want to create in this world? Get your hands dirty. Do it! Not just create some PowerPoint once in a while for some corporate thing, but something real and meaningful that you consider art for yourself. Whatever that is, even if it is a PowerPoint presentation. But to do something that you find artistic and meaningful, that's our human drive for creative expression.

Then, what about contribution? What's your ambition to give and to serve greatly for others? What do you really want to give back or give to others? What is it? And what about connection? The ultimate ambition and aim to have, I think for a lot of people, is their relationships. To operate and to have a love that knows no bounds, a love that is extraordinary, that is amazing. You can't improve your relationship with your family, or your spouse, or those that you serve unless you have, in some sense, that desire to love or give or connect more. So today, get clear. What is it you want? And is it big enough for yourself? Not limiting yourself based on your inadequacies or your competencies, but based on what you truly desire.

Last challenge: Take whatever that is that you come up with and 10X it. Take it by 10 times. What would be 10 times that ambition? Not just because it's silly, I know it's kind of silly, but to take that ambition that you initially have, what we usually want is an impulse based on who we are today.

I challenge you to think bigger for yourself. Because you are immense. You are magnificent, you are a more powerful being than your current understanding. So break through to another level. Challenge your brain to think even bigger for yourself, even as just an activity to break the bounds of your current beliefs and behaviors. You deserve something extraordinary in your life, but first, you have to want it."

DO THIS TODAY: What would the bigger thinking, 10X version of you be doing right now? What kind of goals would you have for yourself? Write them down feel the confidence jump off the page. #254Action

Day 218:
Robin Sharma

"If you're human, you're going to face fear. So one of the things that A-Players do, that leaders without titles do, that iconic human beings do, is they develop a resilience or a hardiness in the face of fear.

In a story I remember reading in an Osho book a while ago, there was this mountain climber who reached the summit of this mountain, but he misjudged the timing and it became dark, so he made his way down the mountain as the sun set, but he got to a place where it got so dark he couldn't move, and he thought he was on this ledge, and he just became paralyzed by fear. He just realized if he moved a few inches over, he would fall thousands and thousands of meters or feet to his death, and so, all night, that was the most terrifying night of his life. He was on this ledge, he couldn't even move forward because he thought he'd fall. He just stayed there, frozen, for hours and hours and hours. Then, with the first rays of daylight, he started to laugh. He realized just below the ledge there was this huge stone platform, there was no danger whatsoever. It was just his perception of fear that caused him to feel terrified.

I think that's a powerful idea for us. The things that most frighten us, when we actually have the courage to do them, dissolve."

DO THIS TODAY: Think about one thing that you're afraid to do right now. Then find a way to do it this week and release the fear. #254Action

Day 219:

Joel Osteen

"There's a large company that has a slogan that says, 'That was easy.' A few years ago, a friend of mine sent me their big red button. When you push it, it says 'That was easy,' and I keep this by my bathroom sink there on the counter. Every so often I reach over and push this button. I like to get that phrase down in my spirit because it's easy to go through life looking at our problems, focused on our obstacles, thinking, 'Aw man, this is going to be so hard. I dread dealing with this. It's never going to work out.' That mindset is not only stealing our joy but it's keeping us from seeing God's favor.

When my dad went to be with the Lord and I first started ministering, it took everything I had to write a message for that weekend. All my focus, my creativity, my energy. I was pressured, stressed. When I finally finished, I felt like that's the last one that I could ever do, and if I wasn't careful, I was tempted to dread it and think this is too hard, I'm not going to know what to say, I can't do this anymore. I had to turn it around. Father, thank you that your yoke is easy, thank you that I'm well able, thank you that you've equipped me and empowered me. I've got my mind going in the right direction. I went through seasons of struggle, strain, and difficulty, but I didn't let it become permanent in my thinking. One day I came into this anointing of ease. What once was a struggle is not a struggle anymore. Every week when I finish a message, I hit this button. 'That was easy.' Just to remind me that it was easy. Quit telling yourself 'This is so hard, I'll never accomplish my dreams, I'll never get out of debt.' This is a new day."

DO THIS TODAY: What are you telling yourself is so hard to do right now? Write down what the first, simplest, easiest step would be to just get started and build momentum. Do that first step today! #254Action

Day 220:
Evan Carmichael

"Remember your why. When you have a big mission, when you're on an important journey, it's just so much easier to get up and do something about it. I make videos because I want to have an impact. I learn from them myself, I love watching successful entrepreneurs, hearing their mindsets, and the way they think, and it always makes me better, and I like making content that helps you guys grow and build better businesses. I feel like if I could have a tiny impact on your businesses, then you're off doing amazing things, that's huge impact.

Remembering that gets me to take action consistently. It gets me to follow through. Waking up today to go and film videos, not because I love standing in front of lights and standing of front of a camera with my cameraman. It's because thousands, hundreds of thousands, millions of people are going to watch these videos, and I know that that's a big impact. So if I don't wake up and I don't come here and I don't do the filming, then I'm not having the impact that I want to have.

So remember your why. I don't wake up super excited. I wake up, and I remember what I'm trying to do today. That really helps me take persistent action."

DO THIS TODAY: What's your why? Can you articulate it? Can you write it down in a sentence? If not, get some clarity on that today. Spend time thinking about it. The more clear you are on your why, the easier it will be to be more confident in your daily decisions. #254Action

Day 221:
Sylvester Stallone

"I think that personal ambition is worth fighting for. It really is something that if you don't fight for it you're going to regret it for the rest of your life, and if you regret it you can be an unhappy person. If you're an unhappy person it's going to affect your family. So you can see the chain of command all the way down, that it can be pretty devastating. The common answer is we fight for our family, but fighting for family starts with you.

So you've got to fight for peace of mind. That's what I think you have to go for, what makes you happy enough in your life that you want to make other people happy?"

DO THIS TODAY: Do one thing today that makes you happy and will make someone else happy as well. #254Action

Day 221 High Five!

If you deal two cards from a deck of 52, you have a one in 221 chance of getting two aces. Personal growth doesn't work that way. Your effort, daily, is helping you turn whatever hand you were dealt growing up into aces going forward. High Five!

Day 222:

Dan Lok

"I was getting beat up in school. I was getting bullied, and I was getting beat up. Not always physical, but I got beat up multiple times. And I was just sick and tired of it. One night I was watching cable TV. I was flipping through the channels, and I saw this guy, and the movie was Return Of The Dragon by Bruce Lee. He was doing Wing Chun, and kicking everyone's ass. And at the end, he fought with Chuck Norris, and then beat Chuck Norris. And I was like, 'Oh my God.' I found my hero. From that moment, you know what? I want to be like Bruce Lee. I want to learn martial arts.

Back then, by my house there was a karate school and I immediately joined the class. I was practicing, I was stretching, I was practicing every day. I was obsessed. I mean, I would practice three, four hours every day, because I was so skinny. I was 105 pounds, but then, I would do my pushups, and workout, and I started gaining a little bit of muscle.

Now, if you've ever done any martial art, you know, after you practice a martial art you develop this natural self-confidence. Not cockiness, but you develop this natural self-confidence. You know you could take care of yourself. So I was doing that.

And I have a teacher's heart. Other kids would start asking me, 'Oh, what are you doing?' I would show them different moves, and as I was showing them different moves, other kids would see us, and say 'Oh this is cool. What are you doing?' I said, 'Well, Chinese Kung Fu.' Every single lunch I would eat for about five, ten minutes, eat a sandwich. The rest of the lunch I was teaching. I was teaching them martial arts, every single day. And I loved it, not because I was teaching them how to hurt people, or even how to defend themselves.

But I noticed the kids that I was teaching, even though my martial arts wasn't particularly that good back then, I could see them transforming. They became more confident, and they became a better version of themselves, and I love seeing people just transform like that.

That's why I owe a lot of what I have today, my character, and my personality, a lot of that came from martial arts. There's no doubt in my mind. As a businessman, as an entrepreneur, as a husband, a lot of philosophies I learned from martial arts."

DO THIS TODAY: Watch my Bruce Lee Top 10 Rules for Success video on YouTube. Rule number 10 has the fight scene with Chuck Norris. You might get inspired too! Here's the link: https://www.youtube.com/watch?v=u7tL8fK6tjA #254Action

Day 223:
Mark Cuban

"The passion I've always had for business and being an entrepreneur, that transfers into the Mavs. I've always been passionate. Some people thought it's more OCD than anything else, which I think is a great trait for an entrepreneur. In the stamp business, I would stay up until three or four in the morning even though I had to get up and go to school and read Linn's Stamp News and Scott stamp journals and have them all memorized and use that to give myself an edge. Even when I was in college, I'd be in the library reading business books looking for business biographies and reading all I could about business. When I had MicroSolutions and I started with no money, I'd pull all-nighters in front of borrowed computers teaching myself software and how to program."

DO THIS TODAY: Study someone or something today that will give you more confidence on the thing you're trying to improve on. Spend at least 30 minutes diving deeper to understand the topic better. #254Action

Day 224:

Mark Zuckerberg

"It wasn't so long ago that I was a student listening to when Bill Gates came to talk at Harvard, and I just thought, 'Wow, how do you do that?' But the trick is that the media likes to sensationalize this: You have some eureka moment, or you are some singular person who built something on your own. That's just not how the world works.

When I was in school, I built a lot of stuff that I just liked building. There was not a single moment when I had some revelation that Facebook was going to be awesome. That's not maybe how the media, or movies would like to portray things. It's much less exciting. But the reality is this: Most services in the world that reach the scale of Facebook start off by building something that you care about, and you don't necessarily think it's going to be that big. I didn't. I built Facebook, the first version of Facebook, for my college community because I wanted to be able to connect with the people at my school.

I remember very clearly talking to my friends at the time and saying, 'How cool is it that we have built this community for our school, one day it's going to be awesome when somebody else builds this for the world, because something like this needs to exist for the world.' But it didn't even occur to me that my friends and I might be able to play a role in doing that, right? Because we were college students. We didn't have any engineers to work with, or servers, or resources, or anything like that. There were these huge companies that deliver products for hundreds of millions of people. I just assumed that it was going to be Microsoft, or Google, or someone else would build this for the world.

What basically just happened is, at each step along the way, we just kept doing the next thing and growing from there. There were teams inside these other companies that thought social media was important and were working on it, but there were all these different memes and narratives in the world. People would say: 'This is just a fad. People are going to use it, but then they're going to stop.' So a lot of the teams who were working on it didn't take it that seriously, or the higher-ups in those companies didn't care, so they didn't get the resources. And we just kept going and going. And then people would say, 'All right, fine. So maybe people are using it, but social media doesn't make any money.' And then we would just keep going and going, and pretty soon, we had a service that was bigger than any of these other ones, and that is how we are here where we are.

There's no magic. A lot of times, I think people just get afraid, because often your dream seems like it's so, so far off. But if you just focus on building stuff that you think is good, and you keep on going at each step along the way, and don't let people deter you from that, and just really care about what you're doing, and don't give up at each step along the way, that's how you build something good."

DO THIS TODAY: Write down your mission. The thing that is so big that you're never going to accomplish it, but you're going to put a dent in it. Then underneath write down what you're going to do specifically in the next three months to make progress on that mission. #254Action

Day 225:

Evan Carmichael

"Upgrade your routine. One of the things that I find really difficult is waking up and having to make decisions. It's really hard every day to wake up every day and decide to do something big.

It's really hard to wake up and have to make a bunch of choices. You get choice fatigue and as soon as you use up all your brain energy to make choices, then you don't have as much energy to make choices for the rest of your day.

So what I want to do is wake up every day and just fall into my routine. I fall into my routine. This is the thing that I do every single morning and that sets me up for success.

I challenge you to look at what do you do every morning. What's the routine, what's the first thing that you do before you leave to get to your office or go to your home office, or get to work.

From the time you wake up, until the moment that you're leaving, or ready to work, what are the things that you're doing, what are the habits that are in there? Are you listening to a podcast? Are you watching a video? Are you reading books? Are you meditating? Are you hugging your cat on the balcony? Are you praying? What are the things that you need to do to make you feel bold, confident and unstoppable?

Because you've felt those moments, you've had moments of boldness and unstoppable-ness. Understand what led to that, what triggered that and then put that in your morning routine. Because if you wake up and you do this routine and you do this every day and it makes you feel bold and unstoppable, when you're feeling that power, you're going to want to take action.

When you watch an inspiring video, you're going to want to do something. When you read a page from this book you're going to want to take some action on it. So what I love doing is not having to convince myself every morning to do something. I just fall into it because I've created a morning routine that sets me up for success."

DO THIS TODAY: Evaluate what your morning routine looks like. Stop waking up like an accident and build a morning routine that is designed to make you confident and successful every day. #254Action

Day 226:
Jocko Willink

"People want to know how to stop the laziness and they want to know how to stop the procrastination. They have some idea in their head, some kind of vision of what they want to do but they don't know where to start. So they say, 'Hey, where do I start?' and, 'When's the best time to start?'

I have a very simple answer for that. Here, and now. That's it. You want to improve? You want to get better? You want to get on a workout program or a clean diet, or you want to start a business? You want to write a book, or make a movie, or build a house, or a computer, or put together some mobile application? Where do you start? You start right here. And when do you start? You start right now.

You initiate the action aggressively. You go. Because the idea isn't going to execute itself. And the book isn't going to write itself, and the weights out in the gym, they're not going to move themselves. You have to do it, and you have to do it now. And that means you've got to stop thinking about it and stop dreaming about it and stop researching every aspect of it and reading all about it and debating the pros and cons of it, just start doing it. Take that first step and make it happen. Get after it and get after it here and now."

DO THIS TODAY: Let's end your laziness and procrastination today. Write down your goal. Then write down a possible first step. It doesn't have to be the perfect first step. Write down any first step. Then do it. Build momentum right here, right now. #254Action

Day 227:

Vinod Khosla

"The funny thing is, with enough persistence most things that seem impossible become possible. I'm always amazed at how often you can turn things around. People take no for an answer too easily. It's whether you're trying to achieve a goal like get into business school, or personally for me, my Green Card was the same way. I left the job that had sponsored me but I still got my Green Card even though no lawyer would take me. I became my own lawyer. Got my Green Card without working while I was at business school. And I did it perfectly legally. My strategy was, if I couldn't convince immigration, I'd confuse them, and I did. And they gave me my Green Card."

DO THIS TODAY: Write down what current obstacle you're facing that seems impossible. How would the most confident version of you handle it? Below write down five potential solutions that you can start working on immediately. #254Action

Day 228:
Martin Scorsese

"What do you do when you change how the world thinks of cinema? What's next? Do you keep making the same kind of film? Or if you're a person like Rossellini, you try something experimental. You push further, it's not just experimental for experiment's sake, but you push the boundaries further."

DO THIS TODAY: Write down three ways that you are going to push your own boundaries further. What's next for you to work on and grow through? #254Action

Day 229:
Evan Carmichael

"Change your environment. This relates to routine as well. When you're in an environment that motivates you and inspires you, you're more likely to just want to do work. When you're in an environment that is negative and depressing, it's a lot harder.

You can force yourself to do work, but on the days where you don't have a strong will, you're less likely to do so. I strongly encourage you to look at your environment. Where are you actually working? Does it inspire you to do great things? And if not, how can you upgrade or change it?

If you look at my home office, where I do a lot of my work day-to-day, it's inspiring. I have pictures of people on the wall that may mean nothing to you or may be people you don't even like. But, to me, it's inspirational.

I want to walk into there and just get inspired to work harder. I don't have to think about it. I don't have to do anything. I just walk in and I get inspired to work.

So you're not going to have a mansion on the water that you can walk in onto the balcony and just do that amazing work.

Okay, you're not there yet. That's fine. But what can you put in your office? Where your desk is? Or can you go to a coffee shop or a library or a co-working space? Understand what the environment needs to be for you to have a great day? Then build that environment for yourself.

I love natural light and I hate fluorescent lights. When I took over Toronto Dance Salsa, everything was fluorescent lights. I had to rip it all out and put in other lights so I can actually come to my studio without getting a huge headache. I love getting natural light, so in my home office I have a lot of natural light right where my desk is. I love being able to see natural light coming in from outside. Some people may love working in a cube with no windows. That's awesome.

Figure out what the environment is that allows you to want to be motivated to work and then design that, so that you're spending one day creating your great environment, and then every other day waking up and doing the work."

DO THIS TODAY: Create your great environment today! Write down what an ideal environment looks like and then make one small, physical change to it to build momentum. Today. #254Action

Day 230:

James Cameron

"Just do it. Just pick up a camera and start shooting something. Don't wait to be asked, because nobody's going to ask you, and don't wait for the perfect conditions, because they'll never be perfect. It's a little bit like having a child. If you wait until the right time to have a child, you'll die childless, and I think filmmaking is very much the same thing.

You just have to take the plunge, and just start shooting something. Even if it's bad, you can always hide it, but you will have learned something."

DO THIS TODAY: Take the plunge. Find the smallest possible way to get started on the idea you've been putting off and just start. It's time. #254Action

Day 231:
Terry Crews

"Take action, whatever you want to do, whatever you're thinking about, you will not get it until you take action. Make that move, make it a small step.

If you want a house, go get a rug. If you want a new car, go get some car freshener. Take action, make this thing happen for you and it will happen. Action, action, action.

One thing that I can really attribute to every failure in my life, whether it be personal, financial, any kind of business, it's because of a lack of my attempt to take action. I did not take action, and it changed once I understood the fact that action is the key. It changed my life in many, many ways."

DO THIS TODAY: It's action day! Write down 10 things you're going to do today. Then do them. Feel the momentum and confidence that comes from saying you're going to do something and then actually doing it. #254Action

Day 232:

Stan Lee

"I had done the Fantastic Four, and the X-Men, and my publisher said, 'Hey, they're doing well, do another one.' So I came up with Spider-Man, and I said to him, 'I got this great idea, I want to call him Spider-Man, and he's a teenager.'

So I gave him the idea, and he said, 'Stan, that is the worst idea I have ever heard. First of all, people hate spiders, you can't call a hero Spider-Man.' Secondly, he said, 'He can't be a teenager, teenagers are only side-kicks.' And finally, 'He can't have personal problems, don't you know what a superhero is?' So he wouldn't let me do it.

One day, we had a book we were going to kill called Amazing Fantasy. When you're going to do the last issue, nobody cares what you put in it. Just to get it out of my system, I put Spider-Man in the book, and we sold it, and it was a best-seller. So, my publisher called me a couple weeks later, he says, 'Stan, you remember that character, Spider-Man, that you and I liked so much? Why don't you do a series of it?' And that's how Spidey was born."

DO THIS TODAY: What's a low-risk way you can test your idea and see if it works? Now go do it! #254Action

Day 232 High Five!

It's day 232. Today we're going to celebrate... just because! You're awesome. And you don't need to have a reason anymore to celebrate that. High Five!

Day 233:
Michael Strahan

"We all doubt ourselves. I doubt myself every day. It's a work in progress, and I think the thing about it is not if you say 'I'm happy and I got it, I have the keys to happiness,' but I think there are certain things that you can do that are triggers. So when you realize that, 'Maybe I'm doubting myself,' you can change your train of thought to get back on the positive side. And I think that's what's it's all about. It's no secret formula in a lot of ways, but it's about recognizing when you're doing those things to yourself and how to correct them and get back in line.

I was playing a game against the 49ers, it was a Monday night game, and I had two sacks that game, and I had ten sacks on the year, which is great by football terms, and I was on my way going to another Pro Bowl, which means I was one of the best in the NFL, but I felt horrible. I felt like I was one of the worst players, didn't feel good about myself, and I went to somebody in Arizona who just reinforced that you have to speak kindly to yourself. Treat yourself, say to yourself what you would say to somebody else to encourage them. And that's what I started to do. And the next week, we had a big game against the Cardinals, and it was in my opinion, the best and greatest football game I've ever played at 15 years in the NFL. And I think it was because I truly told myself, 'You can do this, you know how to play this game. You belong in this game.'

And I've had to use that because I wasn't so sure I could be a sports commentator, which a lot of people think is natural for an athlete to be able to do. But it's not, because I'm as scared and as fearful as anybody else, to tackle something new. But I've learned that sometimes I've got to get over the fear of not doing it because I'm scared, instead of not doing it because I can't do it. And I found that I was more just worried about being scared and what the repercussions were, actually more than feeling like I couldn't do something. And now, by taking these chances, I feel I can do anything.

I think once you get to the point where you don't really care about anyone else's opinion, and you truly trust in yourself, and you're willing to put yourself in an uncomfortable position, then you'll find that you'll get comfortable really quickly and you can do things that you never in a million years thought you'd be able to accomplish.

It's all what you think of yourself. It's all what you apply to it. It's all about the work that you put into it. And if you put in all those things and you apply and you really are interested in something, then you can do it. I have no doubt in anybody. Everything is possible."

DO THIS TODAY: Find one thing, that if you do you'll get judged for, and do it. Feel the judgment, eat it, grow from it, and the next one won't hold as much power over you. Inoculate yourself against judgment today and do something you know you'll get judged for. #254Action

Day 234:

Evan Carmichael

"Commit to someone. When you commit to somebody else, you're more likely to follow through. If you have a 9 a.m. meeting with somebody, you're more likely to be there than if you're just committing to yourself, and that's a challenge for entrepreneurs because we don't have a boss. It's all on us to be able to do something, and yes we have customers and we're working deadlines to help them, but there's nobody hovering over you saying you need to show up and be here on time.

As an example, when I was doing my gratitude live stream, I was trying to build a habit of gratitude for myself and see if it worked. In trying to build a morning routine of gratitude, I created a gratitude live stream on my channel. Knowing that every day I was going to have this gratitude live stream forced me to be there. I committed that I would be there and I would feel really bad if I didn't show up. If people showed up waiting for me to be there and I didn't show up, that would kill me, so I went and did it.

Committing to somebody else means you're more likely to follow through consistently. That could be another entrepreneur buddy that you have, it could be a best friend, it could be anybody in your life, or it could be somebody you meet online that you're looking for accountability to pair up with. When you have somebody that you're committing to, you're much more likely to follow through and be consistent, because we let ourselves down much more than we let other people down."

DO THIS TODAY: What goal are you having a hard time staying consistent with? Find someone in your life to hold you accountable and have them pick something they need accountability on as well. #254Action

Day 235:
Elon Musk

"I actually think I feel fear quite strongly. So it's not as though I just have the absence of fear. But there are times when something is important enough, that you believe in it enough, that you do it in spite of the fear. People shouldn't think 'Well, I feel fear about this and therefore I shouldn't do it.' It's normal to feel fear. There'd have to be something mentally wrong if you didn't feel fear. Just feel it and let the importance of it drive you to do it anyway. Something that can be helpful is fatalism, to some degree. If you just accept the probabilities, then that diminishes fear.

When I started SpaceX, I thought the odds of success were less than 10%. And I just accepted that I would probably just lose everything. But maybe we'd make some progress. If we could just move the ball forward, even if we died, maybe some other company could pick up the baton and keep moving it forward. So we still do some good. Same goes with Tesla. I thought the odds of a car company succeeding were extremely low."

DO THIS TODAY: Write down the main reasons why you need to keep going on your dream, even if the odds of it working are low. Refer back to that page whenever you feel low. #254Action

Day 236:
Art Williams

"I believe that desire and will to win is everything. I don't know why I am like I am, but my butt's always burning. There's always something that says, 'Art, doggone it, you're supposed to go for it. Art, doggone it, you're supposed to be somebody, you're supposed to make a difference with your life.'

What does the $500,000 a year person do, that the $50,000 a year person doesn't do? You look at the outside, and study those two individuals, and everything seems to be the same. They both are the same sex, they both are the same age, have the same train, the same positions, the same contract, the same fringe benefits, they both are successful, they work hard, they're good family people, make tough commitments, but what's the difference?

What does the $500,000 a year person do, the $50,000 a year person doesn't do? He pays the price a little bit more, he works hard a little bit more, he's loyal to the company a little bit more, he believes a little bit more, he makes money a little bit more, he saves money a little bit more, if you want to win in these United States, you've got to be tough, and you can't quit.

In building this winning edge, if you want to win in business, you've got to be a leader. Leadership is everything. You show me anything in these United States that win, I'll show you a leader at work. You show me a successful church, boy scout troop, club, football team, business, I'll show you something run by a leader. See, I thought at one time in my life, you had to be smart to win. I used to see these smart people that dressed so pretty, who talked so pretty, and used these big words, they just intimidated me. And I said, 'Art, you can't ever be that good. Why don't you just throw in the towel and go on back and coach football for a living?'

And I found two things out about smart people. I think it's almost impossible for a smart person to win in business in America today, because I find smart people spend their whole lifetimes figuring things out. They're always trying to figure out an easier way, and a quicker way, and another thing I found out about smart people is they just don't get around to doing nothing, and see somebody like Art Williams, everybody said, 'Well he can't do it, somebody like that can't do it.' But he does it.

Almost everybody in America almost does enough to win. They almost get there, they almost are over the hump, they almost have it going, they 'almost' in everything they do. Almost is a way of life for almost everybody in America, but the winners do it. What do they do? They do whatever it takes to get the job done. If you want to become somebody, do it. If you want to go in business for yourself, do it. If you want to become financially independent, do it. I hear too much talk in these United States, everybody can talk a good game. We need people in America who can do it.

What's the primary difference between winners and losers? The winners do it. They do it and do it and do it and do it until the job gets done, and then they talk about how great it is to have finally have achieved something unique, and how glad they are that they didn't quit like everybody else, and how wonderful it is to finally be somebody they're proud of, and make a difference with their life."

DO THIS TODAY: It's time to do it! Write down the biggest excuses / reasons for now taking action on your dream. Then next to each one decide to take action and write down how you're going to handle that excuse. Today. It's time! #254Action

Day 237:

Les Brown

"Think of some major goal you want, or maybe it's one you're already working on and you have experienced a lot of setbacks, a lot of defeats. You've experienced a lot of disappointment. Maybe you've already given up. And maybe you just need a little fire, a little encouragement to get back in the game again.

There are winners and there are losers, and there are people who have not discovered how to win. And all they need is some coaching. All they need is some insight or a different strategy, a plan of action to make some adjustments that will open up the key to a whole new future for them. That will give them access to the unlimited power that they have within themselves. That's all that they need.

Think about something you want for you, that's real for you. That's important for you, that will give your life some special meaning and power. And I don't even want you to say, 'I can do that.' I don't want you to assume that. See, five years ago when I started out in this area, I would not have been able to make the mental leap that I would be up to where I am right now. I don't want you to begin to just psych yourself out. No, no. I want you to be able to say something to yourself that will enable you to maintain a level of integrity with yourself. That when you say this, even when you face tremendous setbacks, it will be a benchmark to keep you in the game. To keep you moving forward and experimenting and readjusting your strategy and your plan of action. Continuously looking for ways to win.

So what is that something? When you've got an idea you want to move on, you might not have the money. You might not have the education. You might not have the support or the resources you need. What is that something that can keep us going, that will enable us to act on our dream? I want you to say, 'It's possible.'

That's all I want you to do when you look at your dream. Just say to yourself every day, 'It's possible.' It begins to change your belief system. See, the way in which we operate is a manifestation of what we believe is possible for us. Whatever you've done up to this point is a reproduction of what you believe subconsciously that you deserve and what's possible for your life.

Before April 1954, the common belief, the universal belief, because it had been tried again, and again, and again, and people had failed, was that man was not physically capable of breaking the four-minute barrier, that he could not run a mile in less than four minutes. That was the belief on the planet, it had never been done. But Roger Bannister came along and he broke the four-minute barrier.

Now here's what's significant about that: Since that time, up to this day, over 20,000 people have done it including high school kids. What changed? Here's what happened when they got on the track: They knew it had been done. There was a new belief about this barrier, about this goal that was unreachable. And those 20,000 people got in a race believing, knowing in their heart that someone had done it, that it's possible that they could do it. And I'm saying that if you know anybody that had some goal, some dream, something they wanted to do, and they did it, then I'm saying that you know in your heart that if someone has done it, then you can do it, it's possible. If someone can make their dream become a reality, then it's possible that you can make your dream become reality."

DO THIS TODAY: Find someone who has done what you want to do. Study them. Learn from them. Look at how they got started. Model their success. Their story will give you both specific strategies to follow as well as the motivation to keep going. #254Action

Day 238:

Jeff Bezos

"I think one of the things that's very important to note about stress is that it primarily comes from not taking action over something that you can have some control over.

I find that if some particular thing is causing me to have stress, that's a warning flag for me. What it means is there's something that I haven't completely identified, perhaps in my conscious mind, that is bothering me, and I haven't yet taken any action on it. I find as soon as I identify it, and make the first phone call or send off the first email message, or whatever it is that we're going to do to start to address that situation, even if it's not solved, the mere fact that we're addressing it dramatically reduces any stress that might come from it.

Stress comes from ignoring things that you shouldn't be ignoring. People get stress wrong all the time. Stress doesn't come from hard work. You can be working incredibly hard and loving it, and likewise, you can be out of work and incredibly stressed over that. And likewise, if you're out of work but you're going through a disciplined approach of a series of job interviews and so on, and working to remedy that situation, you're going to be a lot less stressed than if you're just worrying about it and doing nothing."

DO THIS TODAY: Write down what you're most stressed about right now. Then underneath write five things you can do to take action against it. Then act! #254Action

Day 239:

Tim Grover

"In professional sports, everybody always said, 'Oh, he's the closer,' and they said that's the top level of a competitor.

I always thought that comparing Michael Jordan to everybody else and putting him in a category as a closer along with all the other players, that's an insult. I see what this man goes through. I've seen his preparation. I don't like to use the word legendary with him because he's not a legend. He's an icon. There's a lot of legends out there. There's only one icon.

A cleaner is an individual, what we call a 'don't think' person. They're so well-prepared at what they do. They spend hours and hours of time, years, of getting prepared, so that no matter what's thrown at them, they're going to deliver that end result. Over and over again. Their instincts are so dead-on that no matter what variable, what problem, they can adjust on the fly and they have the ability to get themselves in what we call the zone.

The problem is in order to be able to put yourself in the zone, preparation is the key."

DO THIS TODAY: Are you preparing enough and getting to be an icon in your industry? Set aside time every week in your calendar to practice and prepare so that no matter what gets thrown at you, you're going to deliver. #254Action

Day 240:
Les Brown

"Most people are not accumulating wealth. Most people are living in poverty, most people are living far below their potential. Not because they don't have the capacity, not because they have not even been given authority and dominion over everything on the face of the Earth. But most people are living like they are living because of the fact that they don't believe they can have any more than what they now have.

In the book called 'The MisEducation of the Negro,' Dr. Carter G. Woodson said, 'If you can determine what a man shall think, you'll never have to concern yourself with what he will do. If you can make a man feel inferior, you'll never have to compel him to seek an inferior status, for he will seek it himself. And if you can make a man feel justly an outcast, you'll never have to order him to go to the back door, he'll go without being told. And if there's no door, his very nature will demand one.'

That's why scripture reminds us, 'Being not conformed to this world, but being transformed by the renewing of your mind.' So every day, you have to sell yourself, and get out of your mind, so those old thoughts, that old belief system.

Every day, you've got to sell yourself that's it's possible. To put a new mind in you, you have to get out of your mind. You have to restructure your thinking. Every day you've got to recondition your mind. See, many of us go through life-making choices, thinking they're our choices, and they're not."

DO THIS TODAY: Close your eyes, think about the life you want to build for yourself, then whisper out loud, "It's possible. It's possible. It's possible." #254Action

Day 241:
Terry Crews

"You've got to rid of those haters in your mind. It's all in your mind, it starts there. Then the judgments that you hear and you accept, you start putting that on other people.

So, when the hater tells you, 'Ah man you can't do that,' that's because he's hearing that in his head. If he says, 'You can't lose all that weight,' that's because he hasn't lost weight and he doesn't want to. He's afraid of the work it will take to do it.

It's all fear, it's all hate, it's a wild, wild mix, and it's in your own brain. There are times when I do something so idiotic, in front of a group of people, just so I can get used to getting away from fitting in. I'll just say something dumb, and it's like, who cares? If I wear something dumb, who cares? I walk around with a wig on, who cares? You can't judge me, I have no shame. It's not going to happen.

And that is where I started to think, now I can go and be free. Because there's nothing holding you back."

DO THIS TODAY: Wear a wig out today. Or something that you'd never wear. Or share something you'd never share. Stop being afraid of judgment and people who don't believe in you. #254Action

Day 242:

Travis Kalanick

"If you get to a place where it's easy as an entrepreneur, it's about to get really, really hard. So what you find is, with really good entrepreneurs, they're constantly making things difficult for themselves.

It's pushing. I like to say you push until it hurts, or you want to be always pushing beyond what you're comfortable with. You're sweating just a little bit, all the time, and when that happens, when you're constantly pushing beyond what you think, what you know is possible, you're always sweating a little bit and you're always a little bit nervous. That is the drug of being an entrepreneur.

So when you're pushing like that and you're never really relaxed, then it always feels small. In many ways it feels to me the same now as it did at the beginning. I'm still a little nervous."

DO THIS TODAY: Look at your calendar and find the thing you're nervous about this week. Feel the excitement from it. If you don't have anything that makes you nervous, immediately put something in. That's how you gain confidence and grow. #254Action

Day 243:

Ben Horowitz

"At any point there's a lot of people that just think, this isn't going to work, the market has changed, this isn't a viable concept anymore.

I don't know how much belief I had, but I knew that I had gotten everybody into the bog with me, so it wasn't so much that I didn't want to quit, I wanted to quit every day. I felt like throwing up when I woke up in the morning.

But I'd hired every employee and they all trusted me. I'd raised all the money, I'd talked every investor into putting their money in. I had given stock to my friends and relatives, and they were all excited about the prospects for the company. When it went public, a lot of my friends from high school bought the stock because I was running the company.

I just felt like I could die but I couldn't quit. And, you know, one of horrible things about being founder CEO is it's the one job you really can't quit, or if you do quit you're a punk.

I didn't want to be a punk. So I just kept pedaling. But it was rough running LoudCloud and then it didn't stop there. By the time LoudCloud was two and a half years old, I had sold the LoudCloud part of the business and I had to change it into another business.

The next thing that happened was LoudCloud was going to go bankrupt. So I raised $160 million in the IPO, but we burned through that and we couldn't stop the burn because the customers kept going out of business. We were headed towards bankruptcy.

I had to sell the services part of the business and all the cash point to EDS, and I had to lay off probably another third of the employees. I kept the remaining 80 employees and we became a software company, a publicly traded software company with no customers and no revenue, which was another track. That's when we became Opsware.

But it was good. That kind of stuff, it makes you strong. Five years later we sold to Hewlett-Packard for $1.6 billion. I'm still shocked by that whole thing. I still wake up in the middle of the night thinking we're going to run out of money."

DO THIS TODAY: Get some accountability for following through on your goal. Tell your friend you're going to do it. Post online what you're going to do. You're more likely to let yourself down than others so use that to your advantage today. #254Action

Day 244:
Jocko Willink

"Any type of danger gives you this flight or fight response, so train. Start some training. Jujitsu, boxing, Muay Thai, wrestling, shooting, competing. You get used to those butterflies when you compete.

Train and get used to seeing how that reaction, what that adrenaline feels like and also get used to understanding what the superior action is. Fight or flight. Because sometimes flight is the correct response. Sometimes fight is correct. But what you want to do is to be able to assess and dictate which response you're going to give, and not just do whatever your instinct tells you, because sometimes your instinct might be wrong. Whatever your situation is, people get the fight or flight response to everyday things, too, like public speaking. Rock climbing.

And that's where I say, do these things, train in them. If you want to get good at rock climbing, you've got to get over that fight or flight response when you get up. Go rock climbing, you'll get used to it. You scared of heights? Go start parachuting. You'll get used to it. You're scared of the water? Get worked up and go through swimming and then become scuba certified. Just get comfortable with being uncomfortable."

DO THIS TODAY: Add something uncomfortable to your calendar that you're going to do in the next 24 hours. #254Action

Day 244 High Five!

Day 244. You're 10 days away! This is it... the home stretch... you're at the finish line... let's end strong. High Five!

Day 245:
Quentin Tarantino

"If you get the passion to do it, and you do it, and it doesn't work out? I worked for three years on a 16mm film that ended up becoming nothing but guitar picks. And I was very disappointed when I realized it wasn't any good. But it was my film school. And I actually got away with it really cheap. When it was all over, I knew how to make a movie. I didn't want to show anybody that, but I had the experience. I had it a lot cheaper than I would have gone to film school."

DO THIS TODAY: Do something today. Expect it to suck. You don't have to show anybody if you don't want to... but do something today to build momentum and show yourself that you can. #254Action

Day 246:
Jack Canfield

"One of the functions of belief is taking action. We did a survey of about 2,000 top entrepreneurs and we noticed that one of the things that people who win in that world have is a bias for action. If they have an inspiration, they act on it.

Have you ever had a great idea, talked about it, thought about it, didn't do it and then someone else did it and was successful and you went, 'Darn, I should have done that?' Maybe it was buy that piece of property, we all have that piece of property we wish we bought.

The idea is that taking action is part of law of attraction. See, a lot of people think you can just sit in your room, meditate, visualize having the perfect car, the perfect house, the perfect relationship and then it will kind of just come to you. I always say, unless you live at the bottom of a hill where there's a road, there's probably not going to be a Cadillac showing up in your living room.

So, think about this, the last six letters of the word attraction spell what? A-C-T-I-O-N. Action! Now, there's two kinds of actions that are critical. There's obvious actions, like if you want a certain kind of car you should go down and test drive it, find out how much it costs, see what it costs to maintain it, go test drive it. I like to test drive a car three or four times, stick my head out the window and say, 'Take a picture of me, I'll be back to buy it.' Put it up on my refrigerator, look at it every day. Eventually, those kind of things produce a car. Saving for it and so forth.

There are also things called inspired actions. All of a sudden, you get an inspiration to do something and you didn't know what it was. You don't have a sense of how is this is rationally going to make sense for me to move forward in my life. For example, a friend of mine Dr. Ignatius Piazza graduates from chiropractic school, and he wants to move to Monterey near Pebble Beach where the golf course is, and he says to the local chiropractor association, 'I'd like to join you.' And they said, 'We don't need any more chiropractors. We have one chiropractor for every eight people in this area, it's too many.'

Now, he could have said, 'Okay,' and let the external reality control his internal experience, but he didn't do that. He said, 'I'm going to think about this and visualize it, and believe in it, and something will come that I will do.' And what came to him to do was to take six months before he opened, and knock on every door in every neighborhood, saying, 'Hi, I'm a new doctor in town, could I ask you a few questions?' And his last question was, 'If I have an open house would you like to receive an invitation?' If they said yes, he wrote it down.

Over six months, he knocked on 12,500 doors, he talked to 6,500 people and gathered over 4,000 names of people who said, 'Yes, I'd like an invitation to your open house.' Now when he opened his office six months later, in a town that did not need another chiropractor according to the professionals, his first month in practice he netted $72,000. In his first year in practice, his gross income was over a million dollars.

I was giving a talk and mentioning this story just about five years ago, and this happened about 25 years ago. Someone said, he knocked on my door and he left his card and two years later I needed a chiropractor and I called him because we work with people we know, we've had an experience with. So he trusted his intuition, he took action on it. Other people would have said, 'Oh I guess I can't have what I want.' You've got to be willing to take the action."

DO THIS TODAY: Block off at least an hour in your calendar for CEO time. This is action time. This is nobody interrupts you time. This is you making progress on your goals time. The more of those CEO time hours you can fit in, the faster you'll hit your goals. #254Action

Day 247:
Will Smith

"The nation's first orcish police officer. My best description of 'Bright' would be to think of it as the energy of 'Training Day' meets 'Lord of the Rings.' Which is a little bit baffling but also surprisingly accurate in some ways.

I wasn't confident I could pull it off, but that's what was exciting. It's so wonderfully weird. I was excited about taking a shot. The fact that it was so strange, as an artist, it was fun to get out on that limb and hoping it doesn't break under your feet."

DO THIS TODAY: Take your shot today. That thing you've been putting off because you're afraid... just do it! #254Action

Day 248:
Tom DeLonge

"When I was in the 7th grade, my buddy moved away to Oregon. There was a week where I went up to go visit him in Portland by myself. He was in school on some of the days, so I could shadow him at school or hang out at his house until he gets out of school. I shadowed him one day and I was like, 'This is weird.' So I told him, 'I'm going to stay at your house and wait.'

But in his room there were four things that were very important: A Stiff Little Fingers record, an All record, a Dinosaur Jr. record, and there was an electric guitar. So what I did was, I would play those three albums on vinyl and I would go over and pick up this guitar to keep myself entertained throughout the day for those three or four days that he was at school. Until he would come back and we'd skate at night and do whatever.

That changed my life. Changed my life. Hearing punk rock music and picking up the guitar, something clicked, where it was almost like, there was a bunch of gasoline on the ground and someone flicked a cigarette and it just ignited. It was a chemical reaction that nothing could take that guitar out of my hands from that point forward."

DO THIS TODAY: Expose yourself to something new today. Something you've never done before. Try a new food. Listen to a new type of music. Talk to someone on the street. Take a different route home. Anything. As long as it's different from your normal routine. It could ignite your life. #254Action

Day 249:
Damon Dash

"The one thing you have to really never do is compare yourself to other people. You can't compare your success to someone else's, because a lot of people want to.

That's what social media does to people, looking at people's pages, and you're like, 'Damn.'

If you're insecure, social media could destroy you."

DO THIS TODAY: Go to someone's social media account that you compare yourself to and feel less than. Use it as inspiration. Look at their posts and tell yourself, "This is what's possible. If they can do it, I can do. Thank you for showing me that it's possible." Learn to kick yourself forward, not down. #254Action

Day 250:
Oprah Winfrey

"You have to keep your own self-full. That's your job. I say to my girls from the Oprah Winfrey Leadership Academy that your real work is to figure out where your power base is and to work on the alignment of your personality, your gifts that you have to give, with the real reason why you're here.

The number one thing you have to do is to work on yourself and to fill yourself up and keep your cup full. Keep yourself full.

I used to be afraid of that. Particularly from people who say, 'She's so full of herself. She's so full of herself.' And now, I embrace it. I consider it a compliment that I am full of myself.

Because only when you're full, I'm full, I'm overflowing, my cup runs over, I have so much to offer and so much to give and I am not afraid of honoring myself.

It's miraculous when you think about it. First of all, for me, my father and mother never married, they had sex one time underneath an oak tree because she was wearing a poodle skirt in 1953.

And my dad, to this day says, 'I wanna know what's under that skirt. That's what I wanna know.' You want to know what was under the skirt? They didn't really have a relationship. She wanted one, but, he went under the skirt and then that was it.

One time, under the oak tree. Bam! Renaissance.

That's why I know my life is bigger than that. My life has to be bigger than a moment in a poodle skirt. It's much bigger. The design, the reason why I'm here.

The ability to take care of that, to honor that, to honor yourself, and that which is greater than yourself. That which was the reason for your being here.

There is no selflessness in that. Because only through that do you have the ability to offer yourself, your whole self, your full expression of who you are, to the rest of the world."

DO THIS TODAY: Do something today just for you. Treat yourself. Buy the expensive coffee. Go for a longer walk. Call an old friend. Celebrate with someone. Buy yourself a gift just because. It's day 250. Make it special. You made it this far and that alone is a reason to celebrate! #254Action

Day 251:

Robin Williams

"There's that feeling of pushing the envelope in terms of what people perceive I can do, especially in playing a character. You know these darker, troubled characters. And in many cases, nasty, vicious. And that helps to just push it through, because you're looking at now.

That idea of playing these characters, it's been a great combination. A really good year to just push the envelope. And I think that's always what I want to do, is to try different things and always change perceptions and change the rhythm.

It's basically saying, 'Okay, now we hit it. And then hit a little harder and then back off. And then go berserk.' Like with the stand-up, which is just free-form, and then come back and play something so controlled, like in One Hour Photo. Those are all possible. I was trained at Julliard. I went for three years and left. And then went and did stand-up. But the stand-up is always a great release and then still having that ability to play both, and having that range really helps.

For me, it's great. And having great friends and family. They just make life extraordinary. And a world to still go out and see and learn about, which is most important of all."

DO THIS TODAY: What's your release when you're stressed? Put on a sticky note: "Remember to _____" and fill in the blank with what de-stresses you. Keep the note close by so you've got the reminder the next time life feels overwhelming. #254Action

Day 252:

Eric Thomas

"It's not about being the best motivational speaker in the world. It's about being the most consistent motivational speaker in the world. And so when you watch me, even if you don't like me and you're into motivation, you've got to fool with me. Why? Because I'm on everything.

How do I do this day after day? Dedicating my life to the search for a few more feet. Yes, I'm a high school dropout. Yes, your vocabulary is better than mine, absolutely. Yep, you look better than me, suit asymmetric look. Yup, you got me beat all day, you got me. Grew up on the other side of town, two parents, great network, you got me.

I'm not going to lie, you're way sweeter than I am. You got all the stuff, you got it all.

But you will not outwork me because your height has nothing to do with my work ethic. Your face has nothing to do with my work ethic. Your background has nothing to do with my work ethic. You will not outwork me. On your jet, you will not outwork me. In your Bentley, you will not outwork me.

For some of you, the reason why this stuff isn't happening for you is because you're getting outworked. Come on, call the best motivational speakers in the world, give us seven days, let us go all over the world and speak.

Come on, and while you're in the green room putting on your make-up you will not outwork me. I'm being real, you will not outwork me.

While you're doing photo shoots, I won't, I'm working. Ya'll are being outworked in your marriage. You're being outworked in your job. You're being outworked with your kids. Your kid's in a gang, why? Because somebody's loving on them more than you're loving on them. They're in a gang, because you ain't hardly at home. You're being outworked. You got somebody else in the hood, who got more. They got your kid even more than you got them.

And you're like, 'I just can't believe this society today.' It's not the society, you got outworked. Some dude up the block is spending more time with your son than you are. Some guy on the block is telling your daughter how cute she is, and you're not.

Because you're grinding, you're working. But you thought when I told you 120, I just meant at work. I mean everywhere, you will not outwork me."

DO THIS TODAY: Put a picture of Eric Thomas on the wall next to where you work. Look at it and remind yourself that he's working and you should be doing 120 in your life too. #254Action

Day 253:
Greg Plitt

"Success has nothing to do with potential. It's all about the perseverance of somebody. That will override any endeavor. If you throw stuff against the wall, eventually something will stick.

You guys that have this potential, that dies. What continues to last forever is the perseverance to always show up.

That's what champions do. Every single champion is the same as every ordinary person, the only differential is that they show up to the event every single day. They see failure as a learning curve. They welcome failure. You learn more from failure than you ever will from success.

So showing up and getting knocked on your a**, finding some effort so you stand back up and reface that endeavor, is going to be the overriding factor that makes a difference. How do you know when you're doing those things? The small things in life add up to those big, monumental things.

The small things, it's a character building block. That your name means something, you hold value to your name. If you drop trash from the ground, you pick it up, because that's your responsibility. You hold value to yourself. When you shake someone's hand, you look them in the eye, you give them a firm handshake.

Because you're here for a purpose. Everything you do, you do to the best of your ability. It doesn't matter what you're doing, it's the fact that you're doing it.

So therefore, it means something to you. That's going to build a legacy. You win the title, fine, that title will not get you another title.

What you are trying to build is legacy. Footprints behind you, that leave motivation for someone else to follow. Legacy is built daily, through the character, the willpower, the code of conduct within somebody.

And that's the perseverance. Showing up every single day. That will always achieve your goal. It doesn't matter what you're pulling with, doesn't matter your potential, whether you were born with a silver spoon in your mouth, or how much money you have. All that can be attained if you show up, and you're willing to risk failure for success. That's my tip."

DO THIS TODAY: Whatever is on your calendar today, make it the best you can do. Even if it's boring work, still make sure the work quality is amazing. Impress yourself and teach yourself today that if you're putting time into anything it's going to be the best there is! #254Action

Day 254:

Michelle Phan

"Confidence is like a mental muscle. Like muscle, everyone is born with it, but not everyone flexes it. And if you want your muscles to grow stronger, you've got to exercise. So here are my exercising tips.

Consciously think positive thoughts, especially during moments when you're feeling down. Take a deep breath and remind yourself that life is too short. And you've got to make the best of it.

Listen to music that will lift your mood. A good beat and sound has been proven to help people in a positive way. Music and sound has been known to help the growth of plants. That says a lot.

You want to have a healthy habit of maintaining this mental muscle. But you also don't want to overdo it. Everything in moderation. Balance is key.

It's good to remind yourself from time to time how worthy and how awesome you are. But you also want to leave room to grow and improve. We can all change and evolve for the better."

DO THIS TODAY: Take Michelle's advice: Put on a song that will lift your mood, close your eyes while the song is playing, take a deep breath, remind yourself that life is short and you're going to make the best of it, you're worthy, and you're awesome! #254Action

Day 254 High Five!

You did it!!! This final high five isn't with me. It's with yourself. Go to the mirror, look at yourself, feel the pride that you get with knowing that you just crushed it. You did what most don't. You followed through. You made it. You've grown. You're a new person now. Look at yourself in the mirror. Smile. And give yourself a High Five!

What's Next?

Congratulations on reaching the end! Here's what's next:

1)   If you want to see the videos series of this book, go to http://www.evancarmichael.com/254 and sign up. It's Free!

2)   The lessons here are habits of success. You don't absorb everything by reading it once. Start the book over again. Make it a habit of reading one lesson per day. If you read a lesson a day and take action on what you read it'll change your life.

3)   I'd love to have your help in spreading the message. If you liked the book please consider sharing it with your friends and online so that more people can learn the wisdom here that is essential but not taught in schools.

4)   If you got great value from this book, consider buying a copy for a friend. Some people are making this book a part of their customer service where all new customers get a copy of the book as a thank you. If it made a meaningful difference for you, it'll make a meaningful difference for others and you'll be remembered as the person who introduced them to it.

5)   Most importantly of all, take action. Don't let this book just sit on your shelf collecting dust. Do something. You don't get changes in your life or business by just reading. You get changes by taking action.

I can't wait to see and hear about your progress. You're going to change the world and I'm honored to play a tiny part in your journey.

Much love,

Evan.
#Believe

One Special Acknowledgement

Everything I do is always a team effort. My wife, my family, my team, the #BelieveNation community... everyone always plays a huge role in making my projects come to life.

I don't usually put acknowledgements in my books because there are just too many people to thank in a meaningful way.

Today though I'm going to make an exception. I'd like to give a special acknowledgement to Mark Drager from PHANTA. Mark has been a friend for over a decade and he's the one who suggested turning the 254 video series into a book.

We stayed up late one night talking about it and then met the next day to get to work. Mark put aside other important projects and resources to breathe life into this book.

Maybe this book becomes a bestseller. Maybe we only sell 15 copies. Regardless of the result, I'm forever grateful to Mark for the idea, the push, the belief, the help, and the love.

His One Word is #Extraordinary and I'm proud of the work we did together here. I think it's pretty #Extraordinary. If you found value in this book, send him an email at mark@phanta.com to say thank you and what these pages have meant to you. They wouldn't exist without him.

Thank you Mark. I love you man.

Evan.

About the Author

Evan Carmichael #Believes in entrepreneurs. At nineteen, he built then sold a biotech software company. At twenty-two, he was a venture capitalist helping raise $500 thousand to $15 million. Evan was named one of the Top 100 Great Leadership Speakers for your Next Conference by Inc. Magazine and one of the Top 40 Social Marketing Talents by Forbes. He has been interviewed or featured as an entrepreneur expert in the New York Times, the Wall Street Journal, Forbes, Mashable, and elsewhere. He runs EvanCarmichael.com, a popular YouTube channel for entrepreneurs, and his first book was Your One Word: The Powerful Secret to Creating a Business and Life That Matter. He speaks globally and is based in Toronto.

#Believe

Made in the USA
Middletown, DE
06 April 2021

37082564R00203